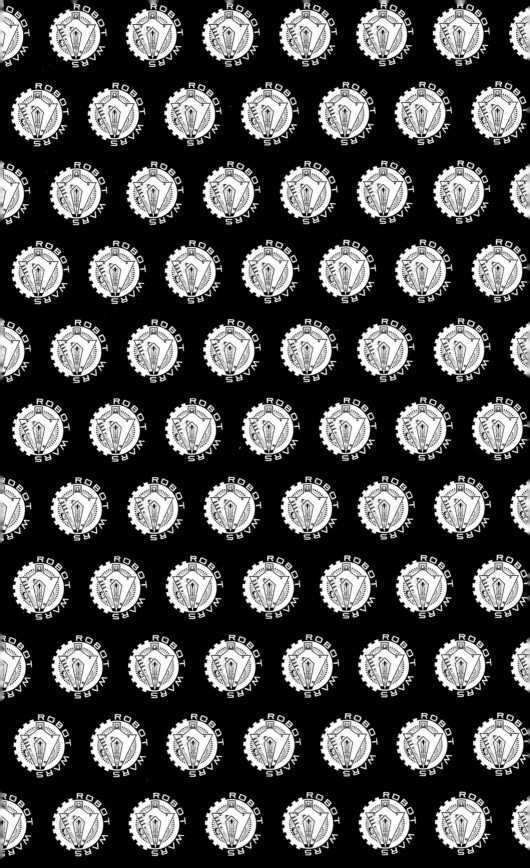

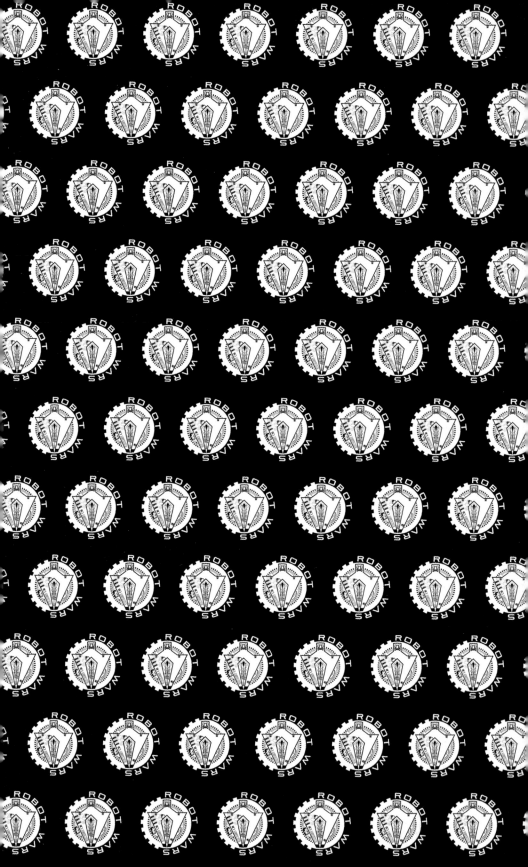

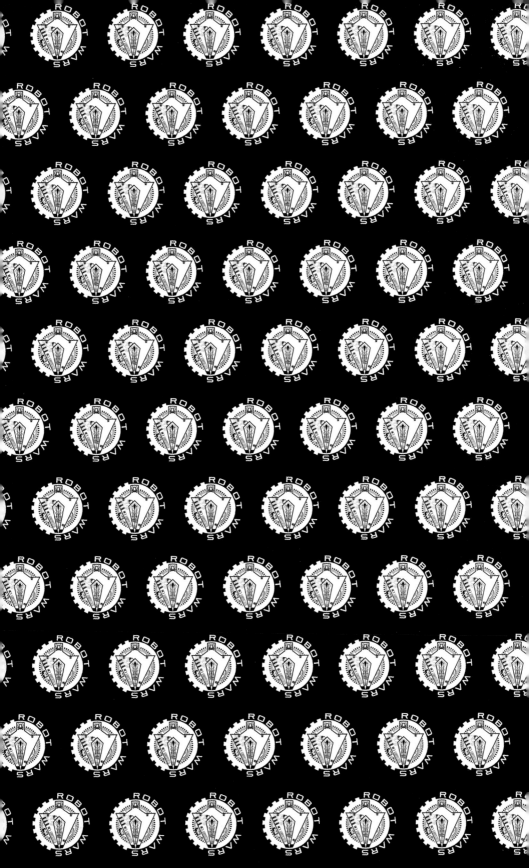

Scholastic Children's Books
Euston House,
24 Eversholt Street,
London NW1 1DB, UK

A division of Scholastic Ltd
London – New York – Toronto – Sydney – Auckland
Mexico City – New Delhi – Hong Kong

Written by Laura Jackson

Published in the UK by Scholastic Ltd, 2017

Trade edition ISBN 978 1407 18470 8
Schools channels edition ISBN 978 1407 18506 4

Printed and bound by Bell & Bain Ltd, United Kingdom

1 3 5 7 9 10 8 6 4 2

www.scholastic.co.uk

ROBOT WARS

THE OFFICIAL HANDBOOK

SCHOLASTIC

CONTENTS

13   THIS IS
ROBOT WARS

19   THE WARS

29   THE HOUSE
ROBOTS

41   ROBOT A-Z
SEASONS 8-10

121   ROBOTEERS,
STANDBY

139   THE BUILD

155   NOTEBOOK

167   GLOSSARY,
ANSWERS
& INDEX

ROBOT WARS

RELAUNCHED

After a long and tortuous 12 years off-screen, *Robot Wars* was rebooted and recharged for Season 8 in 2016. Now the machines are bigger, meaner and more brutal than ever before. You thought the House Robots couldn't get any more destructive? That the competitor bots had reached their peak? Well, technology has evolved, access to learning has never been easier and adrenaline is at an all-time high. The robots haven't been rusting away – they've been evolving. Evolving for the mother of all wars.

With an army of rookie robots charged up for their first combat alongside a crew of old-school bots that are back for revenge, the stakes have never been higher. The robots have never been more powerful. The risk of robot-death never more terrifying. Robot Wars has gone EXTREME!

This handbook is packed full of facts, specs and record-breaking stats about every robot to enter the competition since the relaunch. Read about the winners, the losers, the most destructive, the most entertaining, the most deadly, the bots that couldn't handle the pressure ... they are all here.

Get yourself up to speed with the battle rules and build rules, then plan your own robot design: pick your team, research your power source, choose your weapons. With top build hints and handy tips from roboteers, a notes section to scribble down all your plans, a useful glossary at the back and a complete build checklist, everything is here to help you get started on your *Robot Wars* journey. It's going to be a blast.

SO, WHAT ARE YOU WAITING FOR? 3, 2, 1 . . .

ACTIVATE!

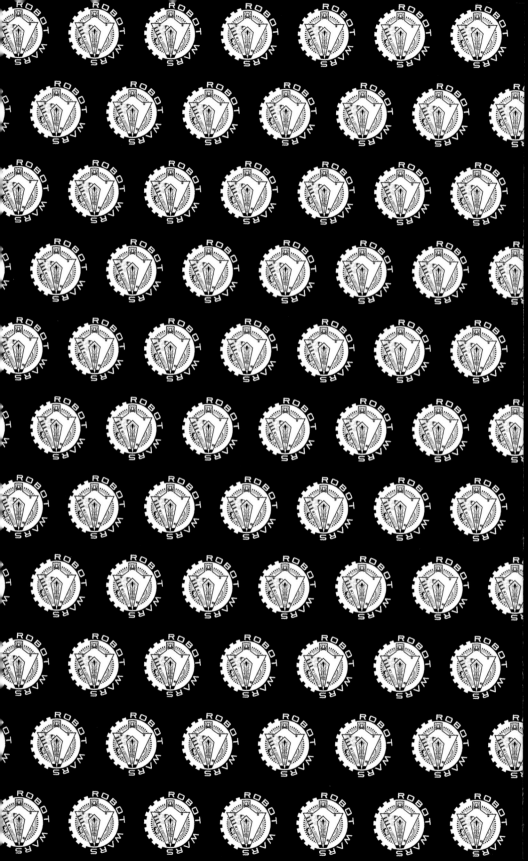

STEP UP TO THE
ARENA

THE FLAME PIT

Evolved for the relaunch, the Flame Pit ignites into flames when a robot is driven or pushed over it. Can cause maximum damage to electrical circuits.

PIT OF OBLIVION

Bigger and quicker than ever, this deadly hole provides instant knockout when a robot falls or is pushed into the pit. One slam on a tyre on the arena wall and the hazard is activated. For Season 10 this will be operated by the Dial of Doom.

VIEWING TOWER

Elevated above the arena floor and protected by bulletproof glass, drivers operate their robots here, safe from the destruction below.

FLOOR FLIPPER

A deadly panel that rises up from the floor and launches the robots directly towards the Pit of Oblivion. Upgraded with more power, it can now flip even the heaviest of bots.

ARENA SPIKES

Five sharp spikes that emerge from the arena floor, with the strength to flip robots over - ouch!

SEASON 10

"Nowhere in our arena is safe for our teams. The spikes, the fire, the flipper and the pit can cut a team's journey short at any time. And the arena just got deadlier.

Pressing the arena tyre now activates one of three random hazards. If the Dial of Doom goes left, the pit opens but if it goes right, it will either release a rogue House Robot who can inflict damage to competitors anywhere in the arena for 10 seconds OR the doom dial activates the brand new hazard...

The Fog of War leads to confusion and chaos as it fills the arena with dense fog for 10 seconds. Competitors can use its cover to turn the tide of the battle, but within the murky mist the deadly House Robots are waiting. Beware! The Fog of War." *Jonathan Pearce, Commentator*

ARENA

STATS, FACTS AND MISHAPS

The arena is the enclosed area where the battles take place.
Rebuilt from scratch for the relaunch, the arena is bigger, stronger and
more than ready to take a beating from the meanest robots on TV!

ARENA STATS

>> 20 X 20 M IN DIAMETER <<

>> 7 M HIGH <<

>> 27,864 SCREWS AND 18,547 BOLTS
USED IN THE BUILD <<

>> 6 TONNES OF POLYCARBONATE
(BULLETPROOF GLASS) IN THE ROOF <<

>> 16.5 TONNES OF STEEL IN THE FLOORING <<

MISHAPS!

Sometimes even the battle zone isn't safe from the robots.
Check out these menacing mishaps...

Season 8, the Grand Final: Carbide vs Shockwave

In a highly charged battle, heavyweight Carbide was carried across the arena
floor by Shockwave. With a final slam, Carbide's spinning blade crashed straight
into the arena wall, taking out a whole section of wall panel. Carnage!

Season 9, the Grand Final: Carbide vs Aftershock

Rammed by Carbide with extreme force, part of Aftershock's armour flew
into the glass wall, piercing right THROUGH the bulletproof glass. SMASH!

TOP TEN ARENA FACTS

1. The floor flipper is powered by carbon dioxide (CO_2) giving it the power to launch 110 kg competitors into the air.

2. The roboteers stand in special booths 2.5 m in the air, which gives them the best vantage point during the battle.

3. The entire roof is suspended from huge cranes. If it is damaged during a battle, the roof can be lowered and repaired.

4. The new Dial of Doom feature selects one of three hazards when pressed. Will the pit drop? Will the Fog of War fill the arena? Or will the House Robots go rogue?

5. When the arena is cold in winter, competitors with pneumatic weapons systems have to store their CO_2 bottles in a warm room before battle. Otherwise the CO_2 is too cold to vaporize meaning their bots have less power.

6. The area around the arena is the Trench, an empty space protected by bulletproof glass where flipped bots go spinning out.

7. The arena wall is higher than ever making it harder for the robots to be chucked out of the battle zone.

8. The seating area for the live audience can hold 400 people.

9. There are three robot entrances.

10. New strobe lighting puts a spotlight on hazard zones and adds a bit of drama to play.

WARNING: BEWARE OF EXCESSIVE NOISE DUE TO FIGHTING MACHINES

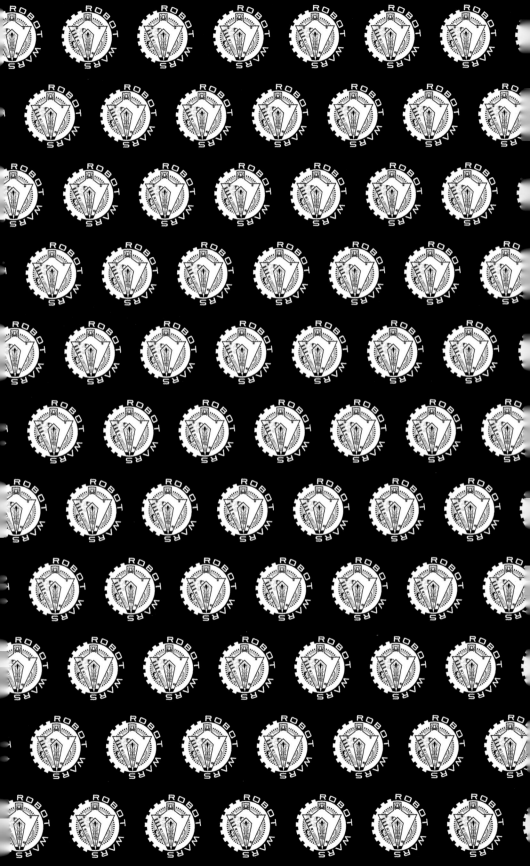

SEASONS 8 AND 9

Robot Wars features 40 teams of robot-fighting
enthusiasts ready to battle to the death in a series of rounds.
Each competitor is aiming to be crowned champion of Robot Wars.
Nobody wants their robot to be sent home in a bin bag.

EPISODES 1-5
THE HEATS

Eight teams and their robots appear in the qualifying rounds.
Each episode is split into three stages:

ROUND 1
GROUP BATTLES

The eight robots are split into two groups of four. Each group
battles it out together in the arena in a three-minute intense
combat. The winning two robots go on to the next round, the
two losing robots are eliminated and are sent crashing home.

ROUND 2
HEAD-TO-HEADS

The four winning robots from Round 1 are thrown back into the arena to face three-minute head-to-head fights with each other. All four robots will battle each other at least once.

Each win gives the robot points. The scoring goes like this: three points for a knockout, and two points if there is no clear winner and the judges have to call it.

The robots in first and second place go through to the Heat Final.

ROUND 3
HEAT FINAL

The two robots with the most points in their head-to-head fights will battle each other one last time. The winners of these highly charged combats will earn their place in the Grand Final.

EPISODE 6
THE GRAND FINAL

Now things really heat up. The Grand Final starts with six teams and their robots: the five winners from episodes 1 to 5 and one wildcard entry chosen by the judges.

The finalists face up to three gruelling rounds of group battles, head-to-heads and a final battle. The winner of the final battle is crowned ROBOT WARS CHAMPION.

SEASON 10

With a new and terrifying order of play, things are
about to get even more intense in the combat zone.

ROUND 1
GROUP BATTLES

Three-way group battles. The winner from each battle
goes directly into the Semi-Final.

ROUND 2
REDEMPTION
KNOCKOUTS

A chance for the losers from group
battles to redeem themselves by fighting
head-to-head to stay in the competition.
Winners remain in the game, losers
are eliminated.

ROUND 3
SEMI-FINALS

Group battle winners and redemption knockout
winners fight head to head. Winners go through
to the Heat Final, losers go through to Round 4.

ROUND 4
3RD PLACE WILDCARD

Losers from Round 3 enter a play-off.
Winners qualify for 3rd place wildcard.

ROUND 5
REDEMPTION KNOCKOUTS

First place goes through to Grand Final.
Second place qualifies for a wildcard entry.

ROUND 6
THE GRAND FINAL
WILDCARD BATTLE

The Grand Final now begins with a mighty ten-way group
battle featuring ALL the 2nd and 3rd places from the
heats in ONE GIANT group battle.

NO COUNTDOWN.
NO LIMITS.
MORE ROBOTS IN THE
ARENA THAN EVER BEFORE.

Ten robots enter. Only one leaves. The winner is the last robot standing, and
it will join the other grand finalists in a battle to become the Robot Wars
Champion.

Prepare for the biggest Grand Final in Robot Wars history!

HOW TO WIN A BATTLE

With so many angry robot-wrecking machines ready to lure their victims to their death, it's important these killing machines have some battle rules. Otherwise the arena would become one smashed-up pit of crushed metal.

DEATH BY KNOCKOUT

Flip an opponent over the arena wall or send it spiralling down into the Pit of Oblivion.

DEATH BY IMMOBILIZATION

Paralyse an opponent for 10 seconds or watch a bot crash out if it breaks down and can't move for 10 seconds.

DEATH BY JUDGES' SCORING

The judges need to step in to call a winner if the battle ends in one of five ways:

The machines become immobolized at exactly the same time

The House Robots unfairly influence the outcome of the combat

There is no clear winner, no immobilization or knockout

There is a health and safety breach

The battle needs to be stopped early

The judges score using three criteria:

DAMAGE

when the robot has
caused clear damage
to its opponent both
visually and internally

CONTROL

showing strong driving
skills and weapon accuracy
through the battle

AGGRESSION

relentlessly taking the
battle to its opponents

SCORING FACT

The judges used to score on 'style' but this
element was removed for the re-launch.
'Aggression' is the most important element
for the modern-day bots!

POINTS SYSTEM

Each of the judges' categories is scored from one to five
and the scores are weighted to show their importance in the wars:

Aggression x 3 | Damage x 2 | Control x 1

CHECK OUT THE GLOSSARY ON PAGE 168 IF YOU NEED MORE INFO ON ANY OF THE SUPER-TECHY WORDS.

THE PRESENTERS AND JUDGES

Introducing the presenting team...

DARA Ó BRIAIN

Joined Robot Wars: for the relaunch in 2016
Favourite House Robot: all of them

ANGELA SCANLON

Joined Robot Wars: for the relaunch in 2016
Favourite House Robot: Matilda

Introducing the commentator...

JONATHAN PEARCE

Joined Robot Wars: at the very beginning in 1998 – a Robot Wars legend!

Best known for: his excitable, loud and downright hilarious commentating style!

Introducing the judges...

PROFESSOR SETHU VIJAYAKUMAR

Professor of Robotics at Edinburgh University. A world-renowned roboticist.

PROFESSOR NOEL SHARKEY

Professor of Artificial Intelligence and Robotics at Sheffield University. The only judge to appear in every show since The First War.

DR LUCY ROGERS

Mechanical Engineer, business and technology communications specialist and author.

THE HOUSE
ROBOTS

HOUSE ROBOTS

Descendants of the original show, the mighty House Robots have been rebooted using modern technology, making them more deadly than ever before. These invincible robots are always on standby, ready to spin, flip, slam and bash the competitors' bots!

THEIR AIM?

To patrol the perimeters of the arena, and attack any bots that are pushed into their control panel zones (CPZ). Their ultimate goal is to immobilize the competitors' bots by causing extreme destruction and carnage. The most-feared hazard in the arena? 100%

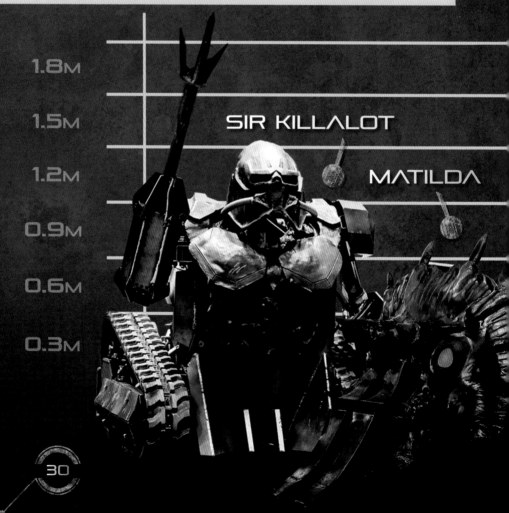

1.8M

1.5M   SIR KILLALOT

1.2M   MATILDA

0.9M

0.6M

0.3M

TOP 5
HOUSE ROBOTS FACTS

1. Not a single part of the original House Robots
was used in the upgraded versions.

2. When Rogue House Robot mode is activated, the House Robots can
leave their CPZs and attack competitor robots anywhere in the
arena for 10 seconds. House Robots off the leash? Terrifying!

3. The House Bots help to save
each other if they get attacked in the ring.

4. Sir Killalot is also known as the 'Daddy of the House Robots'
because of his menacing combat style.

5. The roboteers behind the House Robots had only 3.5 months
to build all four machines from scratch - that is some challenge!

SHUNT

DEAD METAL

THE LINE-UP

ROBOT ROYALTY. WITH A WEAPON THAT WEIGHS MORE THAN ANY OF THE COMPETITORS, THIS CAN ONLY MEAN TROUBLE FOR ANYONE WHO DARES ENTER THE CONTROL PANEL ZONE. BUT NO ONE WOULD BE SILLY ENOUGH TO DO THAT ... WOULD THEY?

WEIGHT	741 KG
ARM LIFT	300 KG
PINCER GRIP	2.5 TONNES
SPEED	16 KPH

WEAPONRY

Drill lance and claws that open to 70 cm wide.
His hydraulic claws have 2.5 tonnes of crush power - ouch!

POWER

Electric; 36 volts (v) with a petrol-driven engine.

SUPER STRENGTH

With a lifting power of up to 300 kg, Killalot can lift up robots
with his mighty claws and crush them, slam them or drop them
in the hazard zones.

ROBOT WARS HIGHLIGHT

His huge tank tracks make him almost impossible to flip. Not that
this stops the competitor bots from trying. After flipping three of the
House Robots, Apollo was determined to get a full sweep and flip
Sir Killalot. But no matter how hard it tried, Killalot would not budge.
He is one stubborn robot!

SAY WHAT?

"Our master of disaster! The lance to chew, the hydraulic claw to cut
through - the nip and tuck, and you're out of luck!"

Jonathan Pearce, Commentator

ACTIVATE THE AXE!

THE ARENA BRUISER, PERFECTLY EQUIPPED FOR PUSHING ROBOTS AROUND. IF THAT'S NOT ENOUGH, HIS TITANIUM-TIPPED AXE LANDS WITH A TONNE OF FORCE, RIGHT ON TOP OF THE ROBOTS' UNSUSPECTING HEADS. BAM!

WEIGHT	327 KG
HARDBOX BUCKET	350 KG
ARMOUR	STEEL
SPEED	17 KPH

SHUNT

WEAPONRY

Titanium-tipped axe firing in 0.25 seconds,
pneumatic lifting-scoop and front-ramming snowplough.

POWER

Scoop and axe powered by CO_2.

SUPER STRENGTH

Built like a bulldozer, he is one hell of a shunter with the power
to send even the heaviest of robots crashing out to their death.

ROBOT WARS HIGHLIGHT

During the final of Season 9 between Carbide
and Eruption, Sir Killalot was getting a severe beating from Carbide.
Using his bulldozer scoop and axe, Shunt slammed Carbide into the
arena gate and stopped the fearless opponent in its tracks. Ultimate
skills in teamwork and damage control!

SAY WHAT?

"A power-packed robot capable of pulling a Land Rover and cleaving all
opponents in two with the sharpened steel axe."

Jonathan Pearce, Commentator

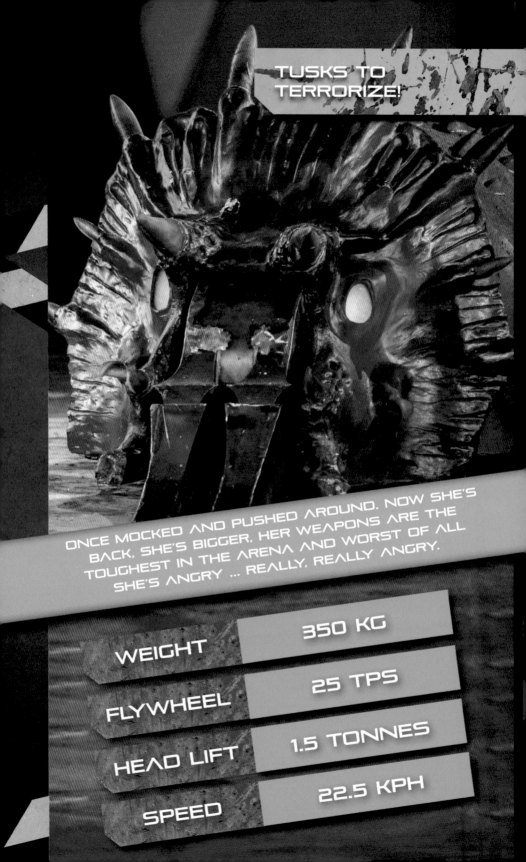

TUSKS TO TERRORIZE!

ONCE MOCKED AND PUSHED AROUND. NOW SHE'S BACK, SHE'S BIGGER, HER WEAPONS ARE THE TOUGHEST IN THE ARENA AND WORST OF ALL SHE'S ANGRY ... REALLY, REALLY ANGRY.

WEIGHT	350 KG
FLYWHEEL	25 TPS
HEAD LIFT	1.5 TONNES
SPEED	22.5 KPH

WEAPONRY

New and improved tusks flip at a force of
800 pounds per square inch (psi) and a vertical
spinning flywheel turns 25 times per second.

POWER

Head is powered by CO_2.

SUPER STRENGTH

New high-torque drive is a force to be reckoned with.
It has enough power to tow a van!

ROBOT WARS HIGHLIGHT

Matilda was the first robot of the relaunch to toss a competitor
into the Trench. With one powerful flip of her pneumatic tusks, poor
King B Remix didn't stand a chance and went hurtling over the arena wall.

SAY WHAT?

"Don't mess with the rear end of Matilda - it's a grizzly place to be!"
Jonathan Pearce, Commentator

METAL MAYHEM

THE MEAN MACHINE OF THE ARENA - BEAUTIFUL TO BEHOLD, BUT DEADLY IN BATTLE...

WEIGHT	350 KG
PINCER GRIP	300 KG
SAW SPIN	340 KPH
SPEED	20.9 KPH

WEAPONRY

A circular saw, which rotates at 4,000 rpm and mighty pincers redesigned to grip an impressive force of 300 kg.

POWER

Battery-powered engine and CO_2-powered pincers.

SUPER STRENGTH

Her spinning blade of steel can cut through ANYTHING. No machine is safe.

ROBOT WARS HIGHLIGHT

Dead Metal made sparks fly when Crazy Coupe 88 drove straight into her CPZ. Slamming the robot into the wall, then attacking with her circular saw, Dead Metal immobilized Crazy Coupe in seconds. What was Crazy Coupe thinking? Dead Metal's CPZ is a no-go!

SAY WHAT?

"It's like watching a surgeon at work only with less blood, more sparks and absolutely no medical qualifications!"

Jonathan Pearce, Commentator

ROBOT A-Z
SEASONS
8-10

AFTERSHOCK

SPIN 'EM OUT!

SEASON 9 FINALIST!

SEASONS 9 & 10

WEAPON	VERTICAL FLYWHEEL
WEIGHT	110 KG
DEFENCE	3 MM HARDENED STEEL
TOP SPEED	22.5 KPH
DRIVE SYSTEM	24 V SCOOTER MOTOR
POWER	ELECTRIC
BATTERY	LITHIUM POLYMER 20 AH
BIGGEST WEAKNESS	BELT AXES COULD CAUSE DAMAGE
SUPER STRENGTH	CAN SHRED ROBOTS APART!
TEAM MEMBERS	2

ANDRONE 4000

SEASON 10

WEAPON	CRUSHER
WEIGHT	UNKNOWN
DEFENCE	FRONT: 15 MM STEEL SIDES: 5 MM STEEL
TOP SPEED	24 KPH
DRIVE SYSTEM	2-WHEEL DRIVE, T64 GEAR MOTORS
POWER	ELECTRIC AND HYDRAULIC
BATTERY	4 X LITHIUM POLYMER, 34 V
BIGGEST WEAKNESS	VULNERABLE TO OVERHEAD AXES
SUPER STRENGTH	8 TONNES OF FORCE IN 5 SECONDS
TEAM MEMBERS	2

APEX

> A SPIKY CONTENDER ON A
> METAL-MUNCHING MISSION

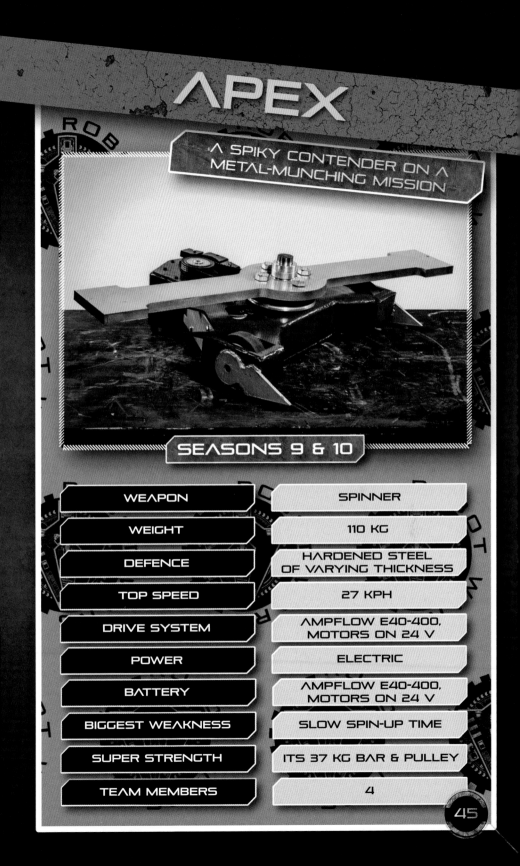

SEASONS 9 & 10

WEAPON	SPINNER
WEIGHT	110 KG
DEFENCE	HARDENED STEEL OF VARYING THICKNESS
TOP SPEED	27 KPH
DRIVE SYSTEM	AMPFLOW E40-400, MOTORS ON 24 V
POWER	ELECTRIC
BATTERY	AMPFLOW E40-400, MOTORS ON 24 V
BIGGEST WEAKNESS	SLOW SPIN-UP TIME
SUPER STRENGTH	ITS 37 KG BAR & PULLEY
TEAM MEMBERS	4

APOCALYPSE

THE STRENGTH OF AN ELEPHANT!

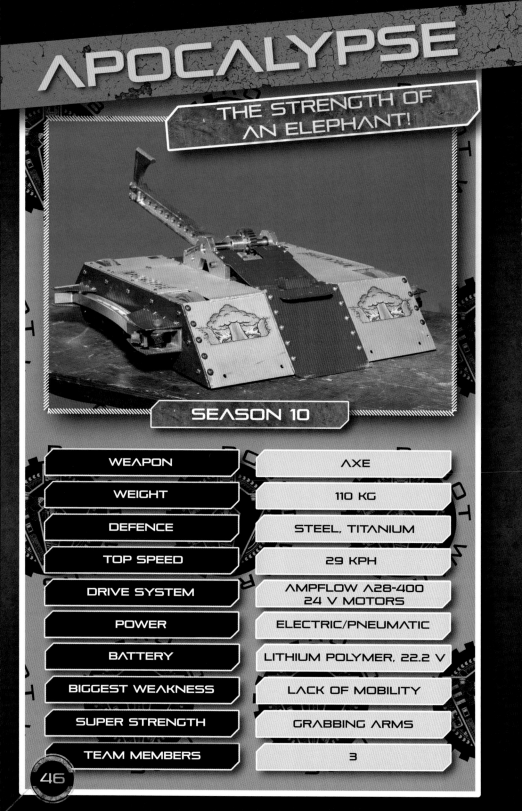

SEASON 10

WEAPON	AXE
WEIGHT	110 KG
DEFENCE	STEEL, TITANIUM
TOP SPEED	29 KPH
DRIVE SYSTEM	AMPFLOW A28-400 24 V MOTORS
POWER	ELECTRIC/PNEUMATIC
BATTERY	LITHIUM POLYMER, 22.2 V
BIGGEST WEAKNESS	LACK OF MOBILITY
SUPER STRENGTH	GRABBING ARMS
TEAM MEMBERS	3

APOLLO

CAUSING A FLIPPING FRENZY
WHEREVER IT GOES

S8 CHAMPION, S9 FINALIST!

SEASONS 8, 9 & 10

WEAPON	FULL PRESSURE RAM
WEIGHT	107.9 KG
DEFENCE	LASER-CUT HARDENED STEEL
TOP SPEED	32 KPH
DRIVE SYSTEM	AMPFLOW A28-400-F48, 11 HORSEPOWER
POWER	PNEUMATIC AND ELECTRIC
BATTERY	LITHIUM POLYMER, 48 V
BIGGEST WEAKNESS	LOW SUPPLY OF GAS AFFECTS THE FLIPPER
SUPER STRENGTH	FLIPPER CAN LAUNCH A BOT 1.8 M INTO THE AIR
TEAM MEMBERS	2

BEAST

UNLEASH THE BEAST!

SEASON 8

WEAPON	FLIPPER
WEIGHT	109.9 KG
DEFENCE	SKELETAL STEEL BARS
TOP SPEED	16 KPH
DRIVE SYSTEM	2 X 24 V MOTORS
POWER	ELECTRIC
BATTERY	2 X LITHIUM POLYMER, 25 V
BIGGEST WEAKNESS	LACK OF ARMOUR
SUPER STRENGTH	THAT FLIPPER CAN FLIP!
TEAM MEMBERS	3

BEHEMOTH

READY TO BULLDOZE
ROBOTS TO THE GROUND

SEASONS 8, 9 & 10

WEAPON	LIFTING SCOOP
WEIGHT	108.5 KG
DEFENCE	7 MM OF GRADE-5 TITANIUM ON SCOOP
TOP SPEED	22.5 KPH
DRIVE SYSTEM	6-WHEEL DRIVE, CHAIN-DRIVEN
POWER	ELECTRIC AND PNEUMATIC
BATTERY	LITHIUM-IRON-PHOSPHATE, 28 V
BIGGEST WEAKNESS	THIN ARMOUR ON ITS SIDE
SUPER STRENGTH	ENOUGH POWER TO LIFT A CAR
TEAM MEMBERS	3

BIG NIPPER

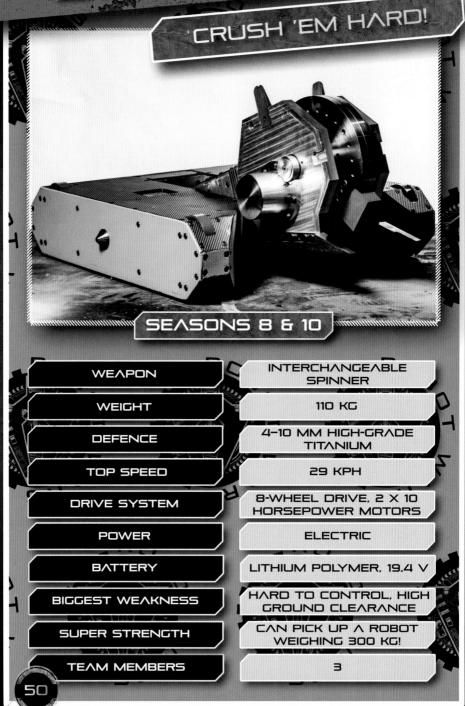

'CRUSH 'EM HARD!

SEASONS 8 & 10

WEAPON	INTERCHANGEABLE SPINNER
WEIGHT	110 KG
DEFENCE	4-10 MM HIGH-GRADE TITANIUM
TOP SPEED	29 KPH
DRIVE SYSTEM	8-WHEEL DRIVE, 2 X 10 HORSEPOWER MOTORS
POWER	ELECTRIC
BATTERY	LITHIUM POLYMER, 19.4 V
BIGGEST WEAKNESS	HARD TO CONTROL, HIGH GROUND CLEARANCE
SUPER STRENGTH	CAN PICK UP A ROBOT WEIGHING 300 KG!
TEAM MEMBERS	3

BONK

DOWN WITH THE AXE!

SEASON 8

WEAPON	AXE
WEIGHT	110 KG
DEFENCE	8 MM WEAR-RESISTANT STEEL AT THE FRONT
TOP SPEED	27 KPH
DRIVE SYSTEM	4-WHEEL DRIVE, POWERED BY 2 X 3-HORSEPOWER
POWER	PNEUMATIC
BATTERY	LITHIUM POLYMER, 26 V
BIGGEST WEAKNESS	AXE IS ONLY EFFECTIVE WHEN BONK IS UP CLOSE
SUPER STRENGTH	TERRIFYING AXE CAN CAUSE CARNAGE
TEAM MEMBERS	2

BUCKY THE ROBOT

CHOMP ON DOWN!

SEASON 10

WEAPON	CRUSHER
WEIGHT	110 KG
DEFENCE	10 MM POLYCARBONATE STEEL
TOP SPEED	29 KPH
DRIVE SYSTEM	2-WHEEL DRIVE, MPC T-64 GEAR MOTORS, 34 V
POWER	ELECTRIC AND PNEUMATIC
BATTERY	LITHIUM POLYMER, 34 V
BIGGEST WEAKNESS	VULNERABLE TO SPINNER ATTACKS
SUPER STRENGTH	A SERIOUSLY NASTY BITE
TEAM MEMBERS	4

CARBIDE

THE SPINNING KILLING-MACHINE

SEASON 8 FINALIST!

SEASON 9 CHAMPION!

SEASONS 8, 9 & 10

WEAPON	BAR SPINNERS
WEIGHT	110 KG
DEFENCE	5 MM MILITARY-GRADE STEEL
TOP SPEED	24 KPH
DRIVE SYSTEM	2 X AMPFLOW 400 DRIVE MOTOR, 24 V
POWER	ELECTRIC
BATTERY	8 CELLS, 33.6 V (DRIVE), 14 CELLS, 58.8 V
BIGGEST WEAKNESS	DANGER OF ENTANGLEMENT
SUPER STRENGTH	ONE OF THE MOST POTENT ROBOTS EVER!
TEAM MEMBERS	2

CHERUB

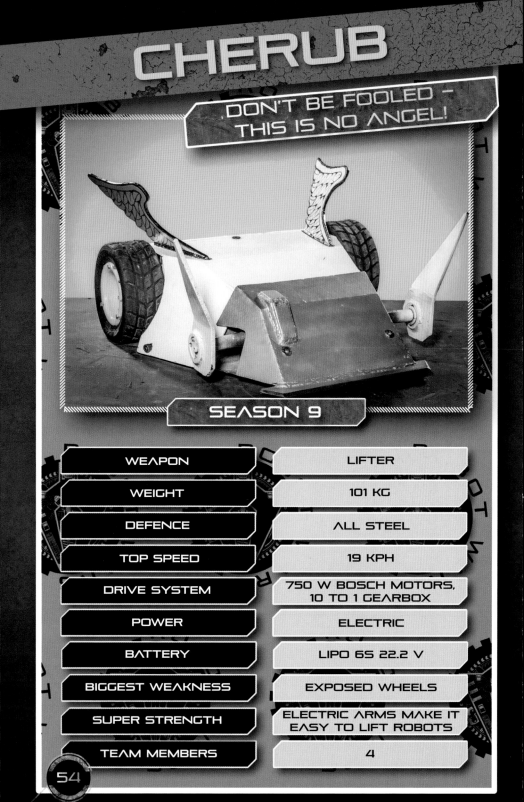

SEASON 9

WEAPON	LIFTER
WEIGHT	101 KG
DEFENCE	ALL STEEL
TOP SPEED	19 KPH
DRIVE SYSTEM	750 W BOSCH MOTORS, 10 TO 1 GEARBOX
POWER	ELECTRIC
BATTERY	LIPO 6S 22.2 V
BIGGEST WEAKNESS	EXPOSED WHEELS
SUPER STRENGTH	ELECTRIC ARMS MAKE IT EASY TO LIFT ROBOTS
TEAM MEMBERS	4

CHIMERA

A 'THWACKBOT' WITH A WHOLE MENU OF BLADES

CHIMERA

SEASON 8

WEAPON	FULL-BODY AXE WITH BLADES
WEIGHT	72 KG
DEFENCE	OLD GAS CANISTER, REINFORCED BY STEEL
TOP SPEED	9.5 KPH
DRIVE SYSTEM	2 X 24 V WHEELCHAIR MOTORS
POWER	ELECTRIC
BATTERY	2 X SEALED LEAD ACID BATTERIES, 12 V
BIGGEST WEAKNESS	EXPOSED TYRES
SUPER STRENGTH	SHARPENED BLADES READY FOR SLICING
TEAM MEMBERS	4

CHIMERA 2

SEASON 9

WEAPON	AXE
WEIGHT	108 KG
DEFENCE	6 MM HARDENED STEEL ARMOUR
TOP SPEED	16 KPH
DRIVE SYSTEM	2 X 800 W 24 V SCOOTER MOTORS
POWER	ELECTRIC
BATTERY	NICD 24 V
BIGGEST WEAKNESS	EXPOSED WHEELS
SUPER STRENGTH	INTERCHANGEABLE CLAW AND AXE WEAPONS
TEAM MEMBERS	4

CHOMPALOT

ONE HUNGRY MUNCHING-MACHINE

SEASON 8

WEAPON	CRUSHING JAW
WEIGHT	99 KG
DEFENCE	6 MM POLYCARBONATE
TOP SPEED	19 KPH
DRIVE SYSTEM	2 X 24 V, 750 W ELECTRIC MOTORS
POWER	HYDRAULIC
BATTERY	4 X LITHIUM POLYMER, 28 V
BIGGEST WEAKNESS	SPINNER ATTACKS COULD DAMAGE ITS JAW
SUPER STRENGTH	CRUSHING MOUTH CAN BITE A BRICK IN HALF
TEAM MEMBERS	2

COBRA

CRUSHER OF DOOM

SEASON 9

WEAPON	CRUSHER
WEIGHT	110 KG
DEFENCE	3.2 MM OF HARDENED STEEL
TOP SPEED	32 KPH
DRIVE SYSTEM	4-WHEEL DRIVE WITH CUSTOM-MADE GEARBOX
POWER	ELECTRIC AND HYDRAULIC
BATTERY	LIFEPO4 36 V
BIGGEST WEAKNESS	BACKSIDE ARMOUR IS FRAGILE
SUPER STRENGTH	CAN PULL A TOW TRUCK
TEAM MEMBERS	4

CONCUSSION

A RECIPE FOR MAYHEM

SEASON 9 FINALIST!

SEASONS 9 & 10

WEAPON	SPINNER
WEIGHT	110 KG
DEFENCE	HARDENED-STEEL
TOP SPEED	24 KPH
DRIVE SYSTEM	NANO-TECH TURNIGY MOTORS
POWER	ELECTRIC
BATTERY	4 X LITHIUM POLYMER 22.2 V
BIGGEST WEAKNESS	EXPOSED PNEUMATIC WHEELS
SUPER STRENGTH	SPINNING DRUM CAN CAUSE SERIOUS DAMAGE
TEAM MEMBERS	4

COYOTE

SEASONS 9 & 10

WEAPON	CRUSHER AND CHAINSAW
WEIGHT	100 KG
DEFENCE	STEEL AND HIGH-DENSITY POLYETHYLENE
TOP SPEED	24 KPH
DRIVE SYSTEM	POWERED BY 24 V, 750 W ELECTRIC MOTORS
POWER	ELECTRIC
BATTERY	LITHIUM POLYMER, 22.2 V
BIGGEST WEAKNESS	CHAINSAW COULD SEPARATE FROM ROBOT
SUPER STRENGTH	THE FRONT JAWS CAN LIFT EACH OF THE TEAM
TEAM MEMBERS	3

CRACKERS 'N' SMASH

DOUBLE THE TROUBLE, DOUBLE THE PAIN

SEASONS 9 & 10

WEAPON	CLUSTERBOT
WEIGHT	110 KG
DEFENCE	5 MM MILITARY-GRADE STEEL
TOP SPEED	29 KPH
DRIVE SYSTEM	FOUR-WHEEL DRIVE WITH 100 MM WHEELS
POWER	ELECTRIC
BATTERY	12S LITHIUM POLYMER
BIGGEST WEAKNESS	TIME IS TIGHT WITH TWO TO FIX IN THE PITS
SUPER STRENGTH	WORKING AS A TEAM, THEY ARE UNSTOPPABLE
TEAM MEMBERS	4

CRANK-E

SEASON 9

WEAPON	VERTICAL SPINNER
WEIGHT	110 KG
DEFENCE	HIGH-PERFORMANCE STRUCTURAL STEEL
TOP SPEED	UNTESTED
DRIVE SYSTEM	2750 W BRUSHLESS OUT-RUNNERS
POWER	ELECTRIC
BATTERY	LITHIUM POLYMER, 44 V
BIGGEST WEAKNESS	THE WHEELS MAY BE VULNERABLE
SUPER STRENGTH	ITS SLAMMIN' SPINNER!
TEAM MEMBERS	4

CRAZY COUPE 88

TIP IT UP!

SEASON 8

WEAPON	FRONT BLADE SPINNER, REAR DISK SPINNER
WEIGHT	101 KG
DEFENCE	3 MM ALUMINIUM PLATE
TOP SPEED	13 KPH
DRIVE SYSTEM	2 X 800 W SCOOTER MOTORS
POWER	ELECTRIC
BATTERY	8 X LITHIUM POLYMER
BIGGEST WEAKNESS	VULNERABLE TO BOTS WITH FLIPPERS
SUPER STRENGTH	WEAPONS AT BOTH ENDS
TEAM MEMBERS	4

CRUSHTACEAN

A CRAB-BOT WITH INSANE SNIPPING POWERS

SEASON 9

WEAPON	GRIPPING CLAWS
WEIGHT	100 KG
DEFENCE	12 MM OF AEROSPACE ALUMINIUM ON CHASSIS
TOP SPEED	32 KPH
DRIVE SYSTEM	TWO-WHEELED 36 V ELECTRIC MOTORS
POWER	ELECTRIC
BATTERY	36 V, 13 AMP HOUR-RATED
BIGGEST WEAKNESS	SPINNERS COULD SEND THIS BOT CRASHING OUT
SUPER STRENGTH	CRAB-LIKE CLAWS HAVE A FORCE OF 200 KG
TEAM MEMBERS	2

DANTOMKIA

FLIPPER FRENZY!

SEASON 8

WEAPON	FLIPPER, SPINNER
WEIGHT	108 KG
DEFENCE	TANK-ARMOUR-GRADE STEEL
TOP SPEED	35.5 KPH
DRIVE SYSTEM	750 W, 24 V MOTOR
POWER	PNEUMATIC
BATTERY	LITHIUM POLYMER, 28.8 V
BIGGEST WEAKNESS	FACING ANOTHER FLIPPER IN THE ARENA
SUPER STRENGTH	FLIPPING POWERS CAN FORCE BOTS TO CRASH
TEAM MEMBERS	4

DISCONSTRUCTOR

MIXING IT UP

SEASON 8

WEAPON	SPINNER
WEIGHT	103 KG
DEFENCE	6 MM OF GRADE-5 TITANIUM
TOP SPEED	24 KPH
DRIVE SYSTEM	2 X 6-POLE AXIAL BRUSH MOTORS
POWER	ELECTRIC
BATTERY	LEAD ACID, 24 VOLTS
BIGGEST WEAKNESS	HIGH OFF THE GROUND MAKES IT EASY TO FLIP
SUPER STRENGTH	RAZOR-SHARP TEETH ON THE SPINNING DISC
TEAM MEMBERS	4

DONALD THUMP

A GOLDEN
THWACK OF CHAOS

SEASON 10

WEAPON	VERTICAL SPINNER
WEIGHT	110 KG
DEFENCE	3 MM HARDOX
TOP SPEED	25.5 KPH
DRIVE SYSTEM	2 X AMPFLOW E30-400, 2.1 HORSEPOWER
POWER	ELECTRIC
BATTERY	LIFE 24 V (DRIVE & LIFTER) 44 V LIPO (SPINNER)
BIGGEST WEAKNESS	THIN ARMOUR
SUPER STRENGTH	AT TOP SPEED IN UNDER 2 SECONDS
TEAM MEMBERS	2

DRAVEN

SEASONS 8 & 9

WEAPON	CRUSHER
WEIGHT	106 KG
DEFENCE	CARBON FIBRE/KEVLAR COMPOSITE SHELL
TOP SPEED	24 KPH
DRIVE SYSTEM	8 X 800 BRUSHED MOTORS
POWER	ELECTRIC AND HYDRAULIC
BATTERY	LITHIUM POLYMER
BIGGEST WEAKNESS	LACK OF FIGHTING PRACTICE
SUPER STRENGTH	JAW CAN GRIP WITH A FORCE OF 6 TONNES
TEAM MEMBERS	4

ERUPTION

EXPLODING FLIPPER POWERS

SEASON 9 FINALIST!

SEASONS 8, 9 & 10

WEAPON	FLIPPER
WEIGHT	109 KG
DEFENCE	3.2–4 MM HARDENED STEEL SHELL
TOP SPEED	19 KPH
DRIVE SYSTEM	2 X 750 W MOTORS
POWER	ELECTRIC AND PNEUMATIC
BATTERY	LITHIUM POLYMER, 18.5 V
BIGGEST WEAKNESS	FLIPPER ACCURACY NEEDS TO BE TIGHTENED
SUPER STRENGTH	FLIPPER CAN LAUNCH A BOT 3 M IN THE AIR
TEAM MEMBERS	2

EXPULSION

SEASONS 9 & 10

WEAPON	SPINNER
WEIGHT	105 KG
DEFENCE	3 MM STEEL-PLATE 'SPACED ARMOUR'
TOP SPEED	8 KPH
DRIVE SYSTEM	2 X 24 V MOTORS WITH WORM GEARS
POWER	ELECTRIC
BATTERY	4 X 12 V
BIGGEST WEAKNESS	NO WAY OF RIGHTING ITSELF IF IT GETS FLIPPED
SUPER STRENGTH	WHEN AT FULL SPEED, SPIKES FLICK OUT
TEAM MEMBERS	4

FOXIC

OFF WITH YOUR SPINNER!

SEASONS 8 & 9

WEAPON	FLIPPER, LIFTER, GUILLOTINE
WEIGHT	97 KG
DEFENCE	15 MM OF ABRASION-RESISTANT STEEL
TOP SPEED	27 KPH
DRIVE SYSTEM	2 X 5-HORSEPOWER SERVO MOTORS
POWER	4 HORSEPOWER MOTORS
BATTERY	LITHIUM POLYMER
BIGGEST WEAKNESS	ON THE CASE TO FIND A CHINK IN ITS ARMOUR
SUPER STRENGTH	'HEAD' CHANGES INTO A LETHAL GUILLOTINE
TEAM MEMBERS	1

FROSTBITE

SEASON 9

WEAPON	BAR SPINNER
WEIGHT	85 KG
DEFENCE	6 MM FROSTED POLYCARBONATE
TOP SPEED	12–16 KPH
DRIVE SYSTEM	TWO-WHEELED DRIVE 24 V
POWER	2 X 12 V NON-SPILLAGE GEL-CAR BATTERIES
BATTERY	MICROLYTE MRT 12 V 35 AMH
BIGGEST WEAKNESS	UNTESTED IN BATTLE
SUPER STRENGTH	FROSTBITE HAS SOME SERIOUS SLICING POWERS
TEAM MEMBERS	4

GABRIEL

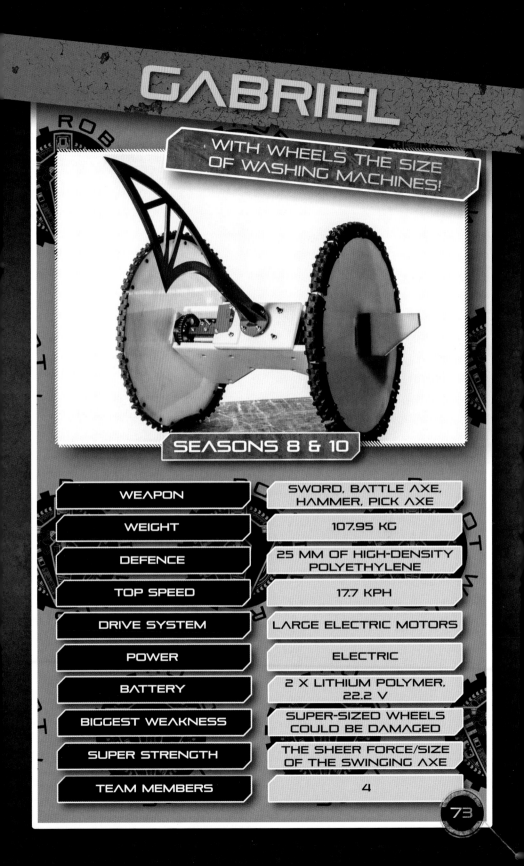

WITH WHEELS THE SIZE OF WASHING MACHINES!

SEASONS 8 & 10

WEAPON	SWORD, BATTLE AXE, HAMMER, PICK AXE
WEIGHT	107.95 KG
DEFENCE	25 MM OF HIGH-DENSITY POLYETHYLENE
TOP SPEED	17.7 KPH
DRIVE SYSTEM	LARGE ELECTRIC MOTORS
POWER	ELECTRIC
BATTERY	2 X LITHIUM POLYMER, 22.2 V
BIGGEST WEAKNESS	SUPER-SIZED WHEELS COULD BE DAMAGED
SUPER STRENGTH	THE SHEER FORCE/SIZE OF THE SWINGING AXE
TEAM MEMBERS	4

THE GENERAL

SEASON 8

WEAPON	RAMMER, VERTICAL SPINNING DISCS
WEIGHT	110 KG
DEFENCE	2.5 MM ALUMINIUM
TOP SPEED	24 KPH
DRIVE SYSTEM	POWERED BY TWO 'ELECTRIC GATE' MOTORS
POWER	ELECTRIC
BATTERY	SEALED LEAD ACID, 24 V
BIGGEST WEAKNESS	EXPOSED TYRES ARE AN EASY TARGET
SUPER STRENGTH	HUGE SPINNING DISKS
TEAM MEMBERS	3

GLITTERBOMB

A PINK MEAN MACHINE

SEASON 8

WEAPON	AXE
WEIGHT	105 KG
DEFENCE	34 MM OF GRADE-5 TITANIUM CROSS-BRACED
TOP SPEED	16 KPH
DRIVE SYSTEM	2 X 24 V MOTORS, 4 HORSEPOWER
POWER	ELECTRIC DRIVE, PNEUMATIC WEAPON
BATTERY	4 X LITHIUM POLYMER, 18.5 V
BIGGEST WEAKNESS	IT CAN FALL SHORT ON SPEED AND POWER
SUPER STRENGTH	ITS PNEUMATIC AXE CAN STRIKE AT 193 KPH
TEAM MEMBERS	4

HEAVY METAL

SEASON 9

WEAPON	ROTATING ARM
WEIGHT	109.995 KG
DEFENCE	STEEL CHASSIS WITH RAEX STEEL PANELS
TOP SPEED	19-24 KPH
DRIVE SYSTEM	BOSCH 750 W BRUSHED ELECTRIC MOTOR
POWER	ELECTRIC
BATTERY	LITHIUM POLYMER 28 V
BIGGEST WEAKNESS	EXPOSED WHEELS
SUPER STRENGTH	ROTATING ARM HAS THE POWER TO CHANGE
TEAM MEMBERS	3

HIGH-5

CLAWS OF DESTRUCTION

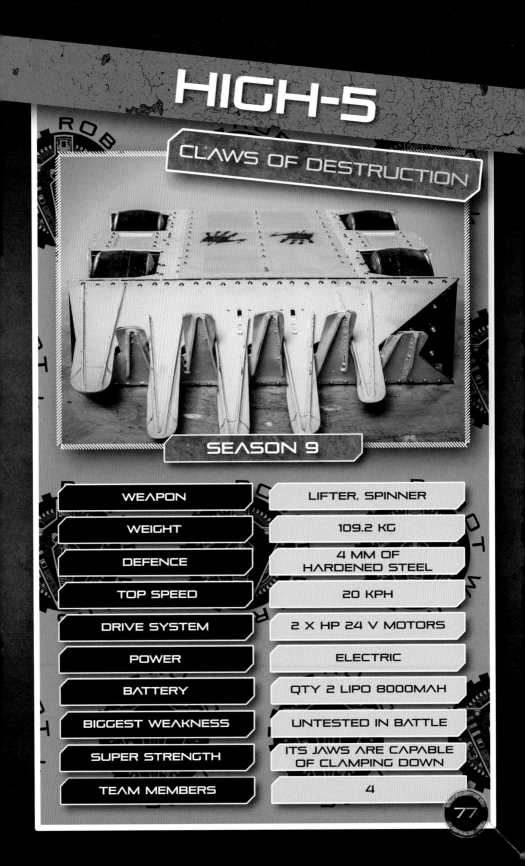

SEASON 9

WEAPON	LIFTER, SPINNER
WEIGHT	109.2 KG
DEFENCE	4 MM OF HARDENED STEEL
TOP SPEED	20 KPH
DRIVE SYSTEM	2 X HP 24 V MOTORS
POWER	ELECTRIC
BATTERY	QTY 2 LIPO 8000MAH
BIGGEST WEAKNESS	UNTESTED IN BATTLE
SUPER STRENGTH	ITS JAWS ARE CAPABLE OF CLAMPING DOWN
TEAM MEMBERS	4

HOBGOBLIN

A UNIQUE DESIGN NEVER SEEN BEFORE ON ROBOT WARS!

HOBGOBLIN

SEASONS 9 & 10

WEAPON	SPINNER
WEIGHT	101 KG
DEFENCE	ALUMINIUM AND HARDENED STEEL
TOP SPEED	14 KPH
DRIVE SYSTEM	2 X 500 W LAWNMOWER MOTORS
POWER	ELECTRIC
BATTERY	DRIVE RUN ON 4 X 6S (22.2 V) LITHIUM POLYMER
BIGGEST WEAKNESS	INABILITY TO SELF-RIGHT
SUPER STRENGTH	ALL-NEW VERTICAL SPINNER DESIGN
TEAM MEMBERS	2

INFERNAL CONTRAPTION

A REAL BRUTE OF A MACHINE

SEASON 8

WEAPON	SPINNER
WEIGHT	86.65 KG
DEFENCE	20 MM OF SEWAGE PIPE
TOP SPEED	UNKNOWN
DRIVE SYSTEM	2 X 750 W MOTORS WITH CUSTOM GEARS
POWER	ELECTRIC
BATTERY	LITHIUM ION PHOSPHATE
BIGGEST WEAKNESS	DIFFICULT TO CONTROL
SUPER STRENGTH	10 MM-THICK STEEL DRUM, SPINS AT 1,000 RPM
TEAM MEMBERS	4

IRON-AWE 6

FLIPPIN' AWESOME!

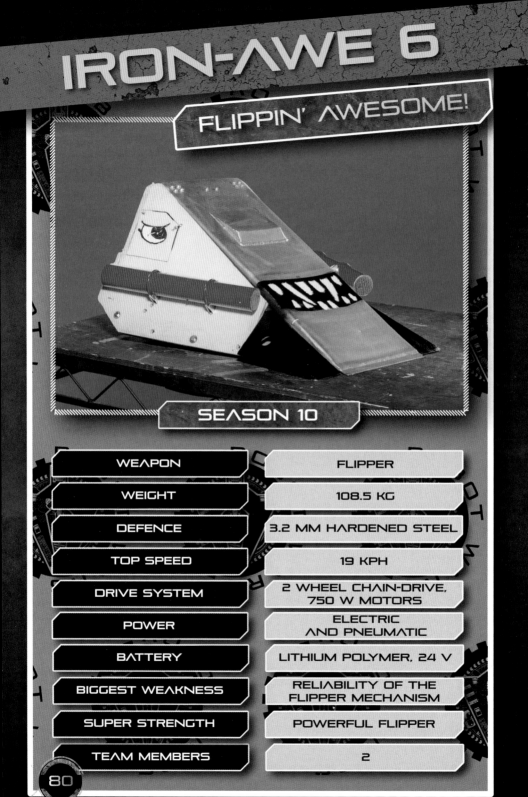

SEASON 10

WEAPON	FLIPPER
WEIGHT	108.5 KG
DEFENCE	3.2 MM HARDENED STEEL
TOP SPEED	19 KPH
DRIVE SYSTEM	2 WHEEL CHAIN-DRIVE, 750 W MOTORS
POWER	ELECTRIC AND PNEUMATIC
BATTERY	LITHIUM POLYMER, 24 V
BIGGEST WEAKNESS	RELIABILITY OF THE FLIPPER MECHANISM
SUPER STRENGTH	POWERFUL FLIPPER
TEAM MEMBERS	2

IRONSIDE 3

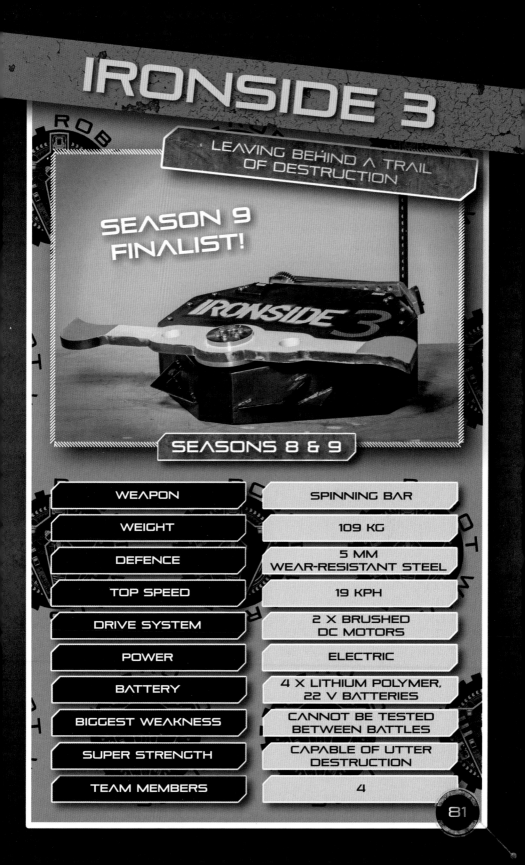

LEAVING BEHIND A TRAIL OF DESTRUCTION

SEASON 9 FINALIST!

SEASONS 8 & 9

WEAPON	SPINNING BAR
WEIGHT	109 KG
DEFENCE	5 MM WEAR-RESISTANT STEEL
TOP SPEED	19 KPH
DRIVE SYSTEM	2 X BRUSHED DC MOTORS
POWER	ELECTRIC
BATTERY	4 X LITHIUM POLYMER, 22 V BATTERIES
BIGGEST WEAKNESS	CANNOT BE TESTED BETWEEN BATTLES
SUPER STRENGTH	CAPABLE OF UTTER DESTRUCTION
TEAM MEMBERS	4

JELLYFISH

BIG, BAD AND READY TO STING!

SEASON 9

WEAPON	CLAMP
WEIGHT	85 KG
DEFENCE	20–100 MM OF HIGH-DENSITY POLYETHYLENE
TOP SPEED	24 KPH
DRIVE SYSTEM	2 X E30-400-G AMPFLOW MOTORS
POWER	ELECTRIC
BATTERY	LEAD ACID BATTERIES, 24 V
BIGGEST WEAKNESS	SURFACE AREA MAKES IT AN EASY TARGET
SUPER STRENGTH	HUGE CLAMPING DEVICE
TEAM MEMBERS	2

KAN-OPENER

RIP OPEN AND CRUSH!

SEASON 8

WEAPON	CRUSHER
WEIGHT	108 KG
DEFENCE	3.2 MM WEAR-RESISTANT STEEL
TOP SPEED	25.5 KPH
DRIVE SYSTEM	2 X 750 W MOTORS, MODIFIED GO-KART TYRES
POWER	ELECTRIC DRIVE AND HYDRAULIC CLAWS
BATTERY	LITHIUM POLYMER, 25.9 V
BIGGEST WEAKNESS	VULNERABLE TO FLIPPER ATTACKS
SUPER STRENGTH	ITS CRUSHER IS THE MOST DEADLY
TEAM MEMBERS	2

THE KEGS

MADE FROM BEER KEGS!

SEASON 10

WEAPON	SPINNING BARS
WEIGHT	109 KG (COMBINED)
DEFENCE	2.5 MM CURVED STEEL
TOP SPEED	19 KPH
DRIVE SYSTEM	24 V, 350 W ELECTRIC BIKE MOTORS
POWER	ELECTRIC
BATTERY	24 V NIMH; 29.6 V LIPO
BIGGEST WEAKNESS	1/2 THE WEIGHT OF A NORMAL ROBOT
SUPER STRENGTH	CAN RIP A HOLE IN A CAR
TEAM MEMBERS	3

KILL-E-CRANK-E

A WIDE LOAD OF SPINNING FURY

SEASON 8

WEAPON	VERTICAL SPINNER
WEIGHT	108.7 KG
DEFENCE	8-INCH PIPE OF 304-GRADE STAINLESS STEEL
TOP SPEED	14.5 KPH
DRIVE SYSTEM	DC MOTORS, WITH TWO-STAGE GEARBOXES
POWER	ELECTRIC
BATTERY	SEALED LEAD ACID, 24 V
BIGGEST WEAKNESS	UNTESTED
SUPER STRENGTH	VERTICAL SPINNING DISK ROTATES AT 450 RPM
TEAM MEMBERS	4

KING B REMIX

SEASON 8

WEAPON	FLIPPER, RAM
WEIGHT	100 KG
DEFENCE	16 MM OF POLYCARBONATE
TOP SPEED	24 KPH
DRIVE SYSTEM	POWERED 2 X 1.8K W HAND-WOUND MOTORS
POWER	ELECTRIC
BATTERY	LITHIUM IRON PHOSPHATE, 40 V
BIGGEST WEAKNESS	CRUSHING ATTACKS FROM CRUSHER BOTS
SUPER STRENGTH	FRONT STEEL SPIKES ACT AS A MENACING DRILL
TEAM MEMBERS	4

MAGNETAR

FLIPPIN' FANTASTIC

SEASON 10

WEAPON	SPINNER
WEIGHT	107 KG
DEFENCE	8 MM HARDOX
TOP SPEED	21.5 KPH
DRIVE SYSTEM	BRUSHLESS SKATEBOARD MOTORS
POWER	ELECTRIC
BATTERY	LITHIUM POLYMER ~50 V
BIGGEST WEAKNESS	VULNERABLE TO SPINNERS
SUPER STRENGTH	CAN FLIP ITSELF OVER
TEAM MEMBERS	3

MEGGAMOUSE

A MENACING TRAP WITH A DEADLY WEDGE OF CHEESE – SNAP!

SEASON 9

WEAPON	FLIPPER, LIFTER
WEIGHT	105 KG
DEFENCE	6 MM OF ALUMINIUM
TOP SPEED	24 KPH
DRIVE SYSTEM	2 X E30-400 AMP MOTORS
POWER	ELECTRIC AND PNEUMATIC
BATTERY	LITHIUM POLYMER, 22 V
BIGGEST WEAKNESS	SUPER-SIZE OPPONENTS ARE A THREAT
SUPER STRENGTH	MINI-BOT, CHARLES, TRAPS THE ENEMY
TEAM MEMBERS	4

M.R. SPEED SQUARED

WITH A BLADE THAT CAN
SLICE THROUGH A CAR

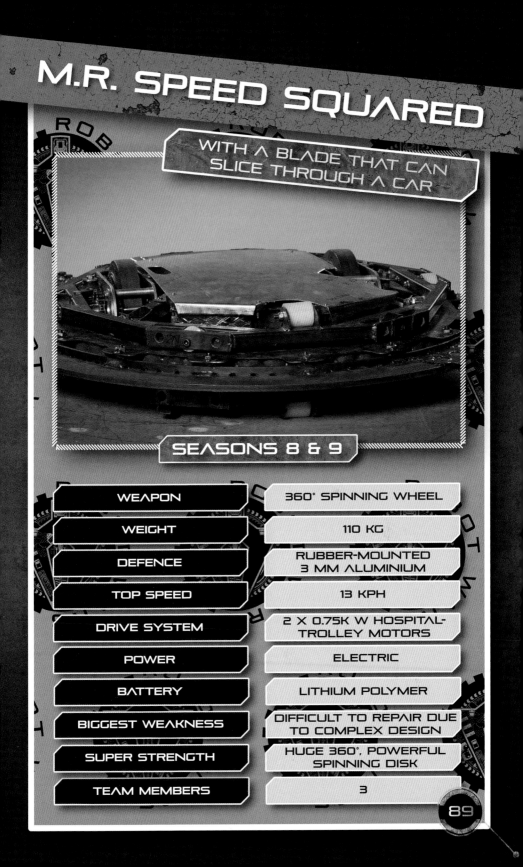

SEASONS 8 & 9

WEAPON	360° SPINNING WHEEL
WEIGHT	110 KG
DEFENCE	RUBBER-MOUNTED 3 MM ALUMINIUM
TOP SPEED	13 KPH
DRIVE SYSTEM	2 X 0.75K W HOSPITAL-TROLLEY MOTORS
POWER	ELECTRIC
BATTERY	LITHIUM POLYMER
BIGGEST WEAKNESS	DIFFICULT TO REPAIR DUE TO COMPLEX DESIGN
SUPER STRENGTH	HUGE 360°, POWERFUL SPINNING DISK
TEAM MEMBERS	3

MS NIGHTSHADE

TALL, UNIQUE AND ARMED TO DESTROY

SEASON 9

WEAPON	SPIKES
WEIGHT	100 KG
DEFENCE	MILD STEEL SHELL ON THE INSIDE
TOP SPEED	UNKNOWN
DRIVE SYSTEM	BRUSH MOTOR USED TO DRIVE WHEELS
POWER	ELECTRIC AND PNEUMATIC
BATTERY	2 X LEAD ACID 12 V IN BATTLE
BIGGEST WEAKNESS	UNTESTED
SUPER STRENGTH	CAN CLIMB OUT OF THE PIT!
TEAM MEMBERS	2

NUTS

WHIPPING OPPONENTS INTO SHAPE

SEASON 8

WEAPON	FLAIL CHAIN, CLUSTERBOTS
WEIGHT	110 KG
DEFENCE	3 MM OF WEAR-RESISTANT STEEL
TOP SPEED	21 KPH
DRIVE SYSTEM	HIGH-POWER WHEELCHAIR MOTORS
POWER	ELECTRIC
BATTERY	LITHIUM IRON PHOSPHATE
BIGGEST WEAKNESS	LACK OF ARMOUR MAKES IT VULNERABLE
SUPER STRENGTH	CLUSTERBOTS PUSH THE ENEMY INTO DANGER
TEAM MEMBERS	4

91

NUTS 2

SEASONS 9 & 10

WEAPON	FLAILS AND CLUSTERBOTS
WEIGHT	110 KG (COMBINED)
DEFENCE	6 MM HARDENED STEEL END CAPS
TOP SPEED	42 KPH
DRIVE SYSTEM	A40-300 GEARED VIA STAGE 11:4:1 REDUCTION
POWER	ELECTRIC
BATTERY	LITHIUM POLYMER, 24 V
BIGGEST WEAKNESS	TOO DANGEROUS TO TEST BETWEEN BATTLES
SUPER STRENGTH	MELTY-BRAIN CIRCUITS SPIN/MOVE TOGETHER
TEAM MEMBERS	4

ORTE

A NIGHTMARE IN METAL

SEASON 8

WEAPON	FLIPPER, RAMMER
WEIGHT	95 KG
DEFENCE	3 MM OF GRADE-5 TITANIUM
TOP SPEED	19 KPH
DRIVE SYSTEM	2 X 750 W MOTORS
POWER	ELECTRIC AND PNEUMATIC
BATTERY	LITHIUM POLYMER, 29.6 V
BIGGEST WEAKNESS	NONE, ACCORDING TO THE ORTE TEAM!
SUPER STRENGTH	THIS BOT CAN TAKE A BEATING
TEAM MEMBERS	4

OVERDOZER

ONE FOR THE PETROL HEADS

SEASON 8

WEAPON	SPINNING BLADE, FIXED SPIKES
WEIGHT	86 KG
DEFENCE	18 MM OF MEDIUM-DENSITY FIBREBOARD
TOP SPEED	16 KPH
DRIVE SYSTEM	2 X DC WHEELCHAIR MOTORS, 24 V
POWER	ELECTRIC
BATTERY	LITHIUM POLYMER, 22 V
BIGGEST WEAKNESS	NO SELF-RIGHTING MECHANISM
SUPER STRENGTH	A POWERFUL PUSHER WITH FIXED SPIKES
TEAM MEMBERS	3

PP3D

A WHEELY DANGEROUS CHUNK OF METAL!

SEASONS 8 & 9

WEAPON	UNDERCUTTING FLY WHEEL
WEIGHT	110 KG
DEFENCE	3-6 MM OF STEEL
TOP SPEED	24 KPH DRIVE, 354 KPH ON THE SPINNING DISC
DRIVE SYSTEM	2 X T64 DRIVE MOTORS
POWER	ELECTRIC
BATTERY	LITHIUM POLYMER
BIGGEST WEAKNESS	THE DISC COULD TEAR ITSELF APART
SUPER STRENGTH	COULD SLICE THROUGH THE ARENA WALL!
TEAM MEMBERS	3

PULSAR

GNASHING AND SMASHING
ITS WAY THROUGH THE WARS!

SEASON 8
FINALIST!

SEASONS 8 & 9

WEAPON	SPINNING DRUM WITH METAL TEETH
WEIGHT	107 KG
DEFENCE	8 MM WEAR-RESISTANT STEEL
TOP SPEED	24 KPH
DRIVE SYSTEM	SENSOR-LESS ELECTRIC MOTORS
POWER	ELECTRIC
BATTERY	LITHIUM POLYMER, 50 V
BIGGEST WEAKNESS	EXPOSED WHEELS WITH ONLY PLASTIC ARMOUR
SUPER STRENGTH	SPINNING DRUM ROTATES AT UP TO 9,000 RPM
TEAM MEMBERS	3

PUSH TO EXIT

ONE OF A KIND...

SEASONS 9 & 10

WEAPON	FLIPPER
WEIGHT	110 KG
DEFENCE	TITANIUM, HARDENED STEEL, ALUMINIUM
TOP SPEED	35.5 KPH
DRIVE SYSTEM	AMPFLOW 24 VDC MOTORS
POWER	PNEUMATIC
BATTERY	28.8 V OPTIPOWER LITHIUM POLYMER
BIGGEST WEAKNESS	NEW DESIGN THAT IS UNPROVEN IN BATTLE
SUPER STRENGTH	THIS MACHINE IS FAST, FAST, FAST!
TEAM MEMBERS	3

RAPID

SEASONS 9 & 10

WEAPON	FLIPPER
WEIGHT	110 KG
DEFENCE	5 MM HARDENED STEEL, 20 MM HDPE
TOP SPEED	37 KPH
DRIVE SYSTEM	20 HORSEPOWER 4-WHEEL DRIVE
POWER	ELECTRIC AND PNEUMATIC
BATTERY	LITHIUM POLYMER, 42 V
BIGGEST WEAKNESS	DIFFICULT TO REPAIR
SUPER STRENGTH	HAS THE STRENGTH TO TOSS A VAN INTO AIR
TEAM MEMBERS	3

RAZER

A SLICE IS NICE!

SEASON 8

WEAPON	HYDRAULIC PIERCER/LIFTER
WEIGHT	109 KG
DEFENCE	2.5 MM OF HARDENED STEEL
TOP SPEED	19 KPH
DRIVE SYSTEM	4-WHEEL DRIVE, TANK-TRACK STYLE
POWER	HYDRAULIC
BATTERY	LITHIUM POLYMER, 12 V
BIGGEST WEAKNESS	ONCE IT FLIPS, IT'S HARD TO RIGHT ITSELF
SUPER STRENGTH	SUPER-SHARP PIERCER CAUSES HAVOC!
TEAM MEMBERS	4

RUSTY

SEASON 9

WEAPON	FLIPPER
WEIGHT	108 KG
DEFENCE	3 MM HARDENED-STEEL EXTERIOR
TOP SPEED	22.5 KPH
DRIVE SYSTEM	2 X AMPFLOW E30-150 MOTORS
POWER	3HP DRIVE, 1200 KG OF LIFT ON THE FLIPPER
BATTERY	22.2 V LIPO
BIGGEST WEAKNESS	UNTESTED
SUPER STRENGTH	RELIABLE FLIPPER READY TO TRASH ITS OPPONENT
TEAM MEMBERS	3

SABRETOOTH

A CHUNK OF METAL WITH A DEADLY BITE

SEASONS 8, 9 & 10

WEAPON	DRUM SPINNER
WEIGHT	109 KG
DEFENCE	3.2 MM HARDOX AND LAYERED HDPE
TOP SPEED	24 KPH
DRIVE SYSTEM	48 V DRIVEN BY VEX BB CONTROLLERS
POWER	ELECTRIC
BATTERY	12S LIPO TURNIGY GRAPHENE
BIGGEST WEAKNESS	SEMI-EXPOSED TYRES
SUPER STRENGTH	ITS 25 KG DRUM SPINNER REACHES 7,000 RPM
TEAM MEMBERS	3

SHOCKWAVE

FINALIST!

SHOCKWAVE

SEASON 8

WEAPON	LIFTING-ARM, WEDGES, SPIKES, SNOW PLOUGH
WEIGHT	110 KG
DEFENCE	4 MM OF ARMOUR PLATING STEEL
TOP SPEED	32 KPH
DRIVE SYSTEM	2 X 4 KW FAIRGROUND RIDE MOTORS
POWER	ELECTRIC
BATTERY	LITHIUM IRON PHOSPHATE, 40 V
BIGGEST WEAKNESS	TOP PANEL IS UNPROTECTED
SUPER STRENGTH	THE ABILITY TO FLIP ITSELF OUT OF DANGER
TEAM MEMBERS	2

STORM 2

A TORNADO OF TORTURE!

SEASON 8

WEAPON	SPINNING DISC, ARM, FORWARD-FIRING FLIPPER
WEIGHT	107 KG
DEFENCE	TITANIUM ARMOUR PLATE
TOP SPEED	19 KPH
DRIVE SYSTEM	ULTRA-RARE EARTH MAGNET PMDC MOTORS
POWER	ELECTRIC
BATTERY	LITHIUM POLYMER, 42 V
BIGGEST WEAKNESS	RISK OF ITS MOTORS OVERHEATING
SUPER STRENGTH	FLIP FROM DOWN TO UP IN 0.3 SECONDS
TEAM MEMBERS	3

SUPERNOVA

SEASONS 8 & 9

WEAPON	SPINNER
WEIGHT	94 KG
DEFENCE	3-6 MM OF HARDENED STEEL
TOP SPEED	19-24 KPH
DRIVE SYSTEM	2 X BRUSHED MOTORS
POWER	ELECTRIC
BATTERY	LITHIUM POLYMER, 12S
BIGGEST WEAKNESS	COULD TEAR APART DUE TO ITS OWN STRENGTH
SUPER STRENGTH	ENORMOUS HORIZONTAL DISC SPINNER
TEAM MEMBERS	4

THE SWARM

THE POWER OF FOUR

SEASON 10

WEAPON	PINCERS/FLIPPER/ SPINNER/ANTI-SPINNER
WEIGHT	104 KG (COMBINED)
DEFENCE	32 MM HARDOX
TOP SPEED	UNKNOWN
DRIVE SYSTEM	RB 775 18 V MOTOR
POWER	ELECTRIC
BATTERY	LIPO 18.5 V
BIGGEST WEAKNESS	4 X THE BOTS = 4 X THE REPAIRS
SUPER STRENGTH	CAN FLIP A MOTORBIKE
TEAM MEMBERS	4

SWEENEY TODD

TIME FOR A WALTZ OF DEATH

SEASON 8

WEAPON	SPINNER
WEIGHT	45 KG
DEFENCE	4 MM OF THICK STEEL
TOP SPEED	16 KPH
DRIVE SYSTEM	4 X 100:1 MOTORS CONNECTED TO WHEELS
POWER	ELECTRIC
BATTERY	LEAD ACID, 12 V
BIGGEST WEAKNESS	IN TROUBLE IF IT GETS AN AXE OR HAMMER SLAM
SUPER STRENGTH	ITS WHEELS CAN MOVE IN EVERY DIRECTION
TEAM MEMBERS	4

TAURON

HALF-ROBOT, HALF-BULL ...
RUN FOR THE HILLS!

SEASONS 9 & 10

WEAPON	SPINNING DRUM
WEIGHT	110 KG
DEFENCE	6 MM AND 4 MM MILITARY-GRADE STEEL
TOP SPEED	19 KPH
DRIVE SYSTEM	2 X 1.5 HORSEPOWER ELECTRIC MOTORS
POWER	ELECTRIC
BATTERY	LITHIUM POLYMER
BIGGEST WEAKNESS	CANNOT BE TESTED BETWEEN BATTLES
SUPER STRENGTH	WEAPON CAN RUN BOTH DIRECTIONS
TEAM MEMBERS	2

TERRORHURTZ

MORE TERROR, MORE PAIN

SEASONS 8, 9 & 10

WEAPON	DOUBLE-HEADED AXE
WEIGHT	106 KG
DEFENCE	12 MM BULLETPROOF POLYCARB ARMOUR
TOP SPEED	17.5 KPH
DRIVE SYSTEM	52 V, 1500 W MOTORS
POWER	ELECTRIC AND PNEUMATIC
BATTERY	14 S LITHIUM POLYMER
BIGGEST WEAKNESS	LACK OF ARMOUR ON THE REAR
SUPER STRENGTH	THE BIGGEST AXE IN THE COMPETITION
TEAM MEMBERS	2

TERROR TURTLE

A SHELL-EBRATION OF TURTLE TEAMWORK

SEASON 8

WEAPON	SPINNER, CLUSTERBOT
WEIGHT	86 KG (TERROR TURTLE), 21.5 KG (THE HATCHLING)
DEFENCE	4 MM STEEL, 3 MM MILD STEEL (THE HATCHLING)
TOP SPEED	8 KPH (TERROR TURTLE), 32 KPH (THE HATCHLING)
DRIVE SYSTEM	WHEELCHAIR MOTORS, ELECTRIC DRILLS
POWER	ELECTRIC
BATTERY	25.9 V (TERROR TURTLE) 28.8 V (THE HATCHLING)
BIGGEST WEAKNESS	THIN ARMOUR
SUPER STRENGTH	SPINNING BAR RUNS AT 3,000 RPM
TEAM MEMBERS	4

THERMIDOR 2

A LOBSTER-BOT WITH THE MOST FEARED FLIPPERS IN THE WAR ZONE!

SEASON 8

WEAPON	FLIPPER
WEIGHT	110 KG
DEFENCE	5 MM POLYCARBONATE 2 MM ALUMINIUM
TOP SPEED	24 KPH
DRIVE SYSTEM	2 X 750 W MOTORS
POWER	PNEUMATIC
BATTERY	LITHIUM POLYMER, 25.9 V
BIGGEST WEAKNESS	VULNERABLE IF ITS SHELL IS PUNCTURED
SUPER STRENGTH	PNEUMATIC FLIPPER CAN LIFT 2,300 KG
TEAM MEMBERS	2

THOR

ʌ STORM OF DESTRUCTION

SEASONS 8, 9 & 10

WEAPON	HAMMER
WEIGHT	105 KG
DEFENCE	3-6 MM HARDOX STEEL
TOP SPEED	48 KPH
DRIVE SYSTEM	MAG MOTORS
POWER	ELECTRIC AND PNEUMATIC
BATTERY	LITHIUM POLYMER, 28 V
BIGGEST WEAKNESS	ʌ LITTLE LIGHT ON THE ARMOUR-FRONT
SUPER STRENGTH	CAN PULL A 2-TONNE VAN
TEAM MEMBERS	1

TMHWK

A CHARGED-UP CHUNK OF GIRL POWER

SEASON 9

WEAPON	AXE
WEIGHT	106 KG
DEFENCE	3.2 MM HARDENED-STEEL ARMOUR
TOP SPEED	UNTESTED
DRIVE SYSTEM	GPA 750 MOTOR
POWER	ELECTRIC
BATTERY	LITHIUM POLYMER 8S
BIGGEST WEAKNESS	WHEELS ON THE TOP ARE PRONE TO ATTACK
SUPER STRENGTH	AXE HEADS FOR ULTIMATE SLICING
TEAM MEMBERS	4

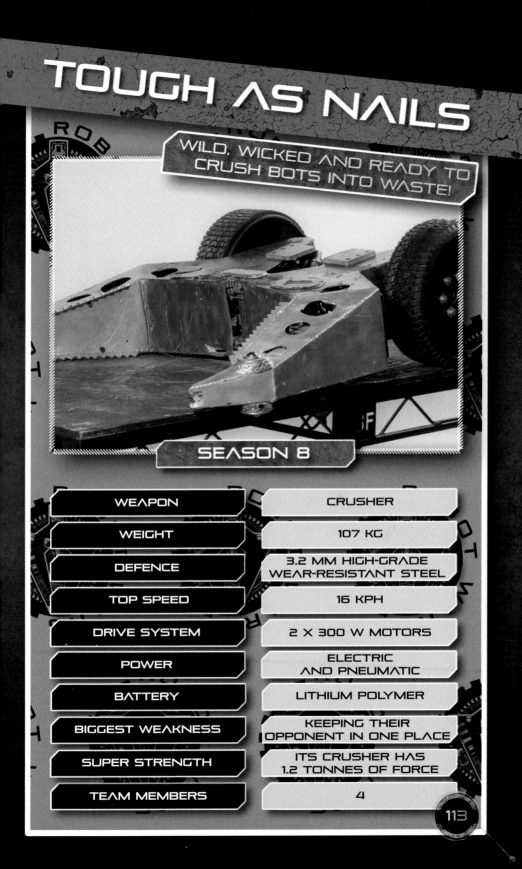

TOUGH AS NAILS

WILD, WICKED AND READY TO CRUSH BOTS INTO WASTE!

SEASON 8

WEAPON	CRUSHER
WEIGHT	107 KG
DEFENCE	3.2 MM HIGH-GRADE WEAR-RESISTANT STEEL
TOP SPEED	16 KPH
DRIVE SYSTEM	2 X 300 W MOTORS
POWER	ELECTRIC AND PNEUMATIC
BATTERY	LITHIUM POLYMER
BIGGEST WEAKNESS	KEEPING THEIR OPPONENT IN ONE PLACE
SUPER STRENGTH	ITS CRUSHER HAS 1.2 TONNES OF FORCE
TEAM MEMBERS	4

TRACKTION

HAS THE STRENGTH TO PULL A MINIBUS

SEASON 10

WEAPON	CRUSHER/GRIPPER
WEIGHT	95 KG
DEFENCE	MILD STEEL
TOP SPEED	16 KPH
DRIVE SYSTEM	2 X CIM MOTORS
POWER	ELECTRIC
BATTERY	LITHIUM POLYMER
BIGGEST WEAKNESS	LIMITED ARMOUR
SUPER STRENGTH	TRACKS MEANS IT CAN RUN BOTH WAYS
TEAM MEMBERS	4

TR2

THE SHARPEST MOVES AND GROOVES

FINALIST!

TR2

SEASON 8

WEAPON	FLIPPER WITH AXE ON ITS REAR
WEIGHT	105.35 KG
DEFENCE	3.2 MM WEAR-RESISTANT STEEL
TOP SPEED	24 KPH
DRIVE SYSTEM	750 W MOTORS WITH CUSTOM-MADE GEARBOX
POWER	PNEUMATIC
BATTERY	4 X LITHIUM IRON PHOSPHATE, 26 V
BIGGEST WEAKNESS	THE WELDING COULD BE IMPROVED
SUPER STRENGTH	AWESOME DRIVING SKILLS
TEAM MEMBERS	3

TROLLEY RAGE

ONE MEAN-LOOKING SHOPPING CART!

TROLLEY

RAGE!

SEASON 9

WEAPON	AXE
WEIGHT	108 KG
DEFENCE	3 MM STEEL PLATING
TOP SPEED	9.5 KPH
DRIVE SYSTEM	2 X 24 V WHEELCHAIR MOTORS
POWER	ELECTRIC
BATTERY	2 X 21 V LITHIUM ION BATTERIES
BIGGEST WEAKNESS	COULD BE IMMOBILIZED BY BIG SLAMS
SUPER STRENGTH	IMAGINATIVE BUILD PROVES TO BE CHEAP!
TEAM MEMBERS	4

WYRM

BUILT WITH THE VERY LEAST AMOUNT OF MACHINERY

SEASON 9

WEAPON	LIFTING WEDGE
WEIGHT	110 KG
DEFENCE	100 MM PLATES OF HARDENED STEEL
TOP SPEED	21 KPH
DRIVE SYSTEM	2 X 100 W ELECTRIC SCOOTER MOTORS
POWER	ELECTRIC
BATTERY	LITHIUM POLYMER, 3 X 3S FOR 33 V
BIGGEST WEAKNESS	MECHANISM CAN BE SLOW, OPEN TO ATTACK
SUPER STRENGTH	PROTECTS ITSELF AGAINST SPINNERS
TEAM MEMBERS	3

VULTURE

PREYING FROM OVERHEAD

SEASON 10

WEAPON	SPINNING BAR HEAD
WEIGHT	100 KG
DEFENCE	6 MM STEEL WITH 8 MM PANELS
TOP SPEED	25.5 KPH
DRIVE SYSTEM	24 V, 1600 W MOTOR
POWER	ELECTRIC
BATTERY	LITHIUM POLYMER 30 V
BIGGEST WEAKNESS	THE WELDING
SUPER STRENGTH	TRAVELS 180° IN HALF A SECOND
TEAM MEMBERS	4

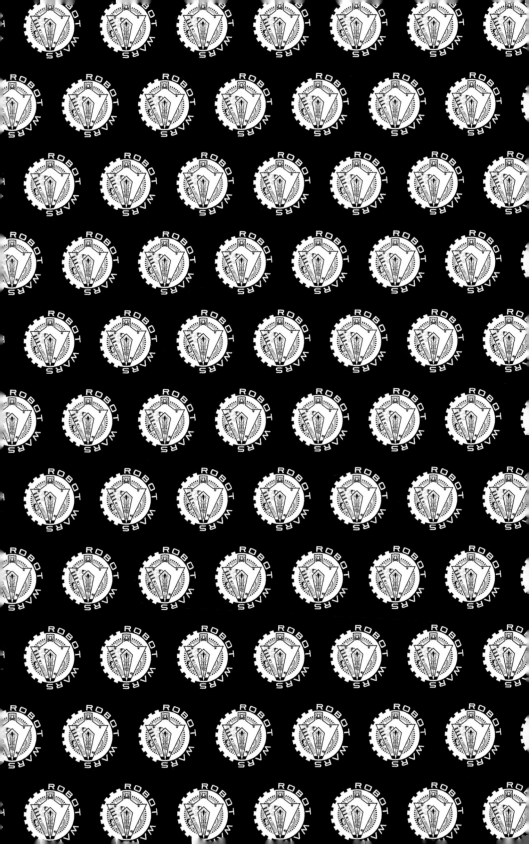

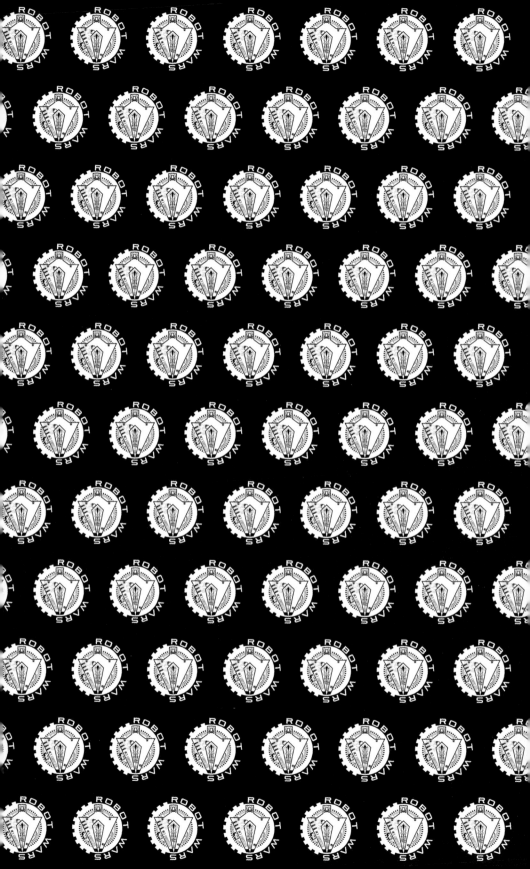

ROBOTEERS,
STANDBY

LIFE IN THE PITS

Backstage, life in the Pits can be tense. Like a hospital for battered bots, competitors are on a countdown to fix wounds, prepare weapons and repair damage. All the while, the clock is ticking and the next battle is always looming. Tick, tock, tick, tock...

TEST IT

The testing area in the Pits is used by roboteers to trial their weaponry. This is their last chance to check that their robots are ready for the metal-munching action of the arena. If things are not up to scratch, it's time to hit the workbenches.

FIX IT

Each team has its own workbench and tools. It's a high-energy area with teams furiously battling to fix their robots between battles.

WATCH THE CLOCK

The roboteers are given a minimum of two hours after a battle to repair any battering that was dished out in the arena. It seems like a long time, but when the teams have to get their robots to and from the Pits, do post-match interviews and sometimes carry out major chassis repairs, it soon becomes a race against time.

01:59

LIFE IN THE PITS IS NOT FOR THE FAINT-HEARTED!

IN THE PITS WITH TEAM ERUPTION

You get a minimum of two hours in the Pits to fix up your bot. What is the atmosphere like between battles?

Usually very frantic, there is definitely a sense of urgency and you can't afford to waste any time.

Do rival teams help each other out behind the scenes or is it every team for themselves?

Despite us trying to smash up each other's robots, all the teams are actually very good friends behind the scenes. Teams are always helping each other in any way they can, even if they are due to be fighting them soon!

If you had to pick only three tools to take into the Pits, what would they be?

An angle grinder as we have to make sure our flipper blades remain sharp for each fight, and to cut away any pieces of damage, which get in the way. An adjustable spanner and a soldering iron in case we need to repair wiring.

Did you know?
Some teams decorate their areas in the Pits. King B Remix added a disco ball to their workbench!

SEASON 8 CHAMPION

The Grand Final of Season 8 was a nail-biting battle between ferocious flipper, Apollo, and metal-muncher, Carbide. Both robots were intent on smashing each other into orbit. It was a match of robot royalty not to be missed.

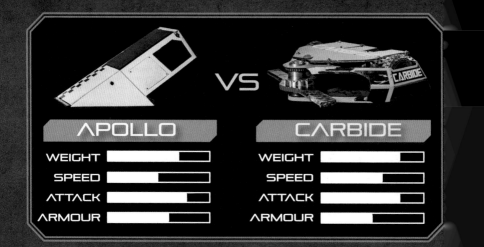

APOLLO

WEIGHT	
SPEED	
ATTACK	
ARMOUR	

CARBIDE

WEIGHT	
SPEED	
ATTACK	
ARMOUR	

VS

Winner:

APOLLO

Dream team:
Dave Young (captain and driver),
Marc Dermott (engineer), Ben Bacon (engineer)

Team Lowdown:
Bluecoats Dave and Marc have been friends for years,
but are fairly new to the world of roboteering.
This makes their success all the more awesome!

Fast Fact
Apollo returned for series 9, but was
immobolized by Aftershock in the Grand Fin

HIGHLIGHTS OF
APOLLO'S SEASON 8 JOURNEY

The Qualifiers: despite suffering a blow to its wheel, Apollo immobolized Kan-Opener, flipped Sweeny Todd and qualified for the next round.

Head-to-Heads: daring to enter Dead Metal's CPZ in a battle with Storm 2, Apollo pulled off the ultimate move by flipping the House Robot. If that wasn't bad enough, Apollo went in for the kill and flipped Matilda too. How rude!

Heat Final: struggling against Storm 2's crazy ground clearance, Apollo was pushed into Shunt's CPZ. Unfazed, Apollo flipped Shunt. Three House Robots down, one to go!

Grand Final: facing the mighty Carbide in the head-to-head was not so easy. Carbide knocked out Apollo's removable link, immobilizing it. Bruised and battered, Apollo was out for revenge. The final battle pitted Apollo once more against Carbide. This time Apollo trapped Carbide under its flipper and drove it into the axe of Shunt. Game over for Carbide!

Did you know?
This was the first ever Grand Final since The First Wars where every competitor that won its qualifying battle was a newcomer to the TV series. The only oldie was Thor, who was selected as a wildcard.

SPEED ROUND WITH
THE APOLLO TEAM

How did the team prepare for the final battle?

Coffee, lots of coffee. Also we normally have a bit of a jump and a dance around. Gets you in the spirit for a fight!

Did you have any tactics?

Try and not leave in a bin bag. That's the only tactic you can have in any fight.

How difficult was it to smash Carbide out of the final?

Carbide was a massive challenge. But we knew its weakness was its weapon. The Carbide disc hits with such a force, but half of that force has to go back into their robot too. If you can keep taking the hits, it's a 50/50 chance who will give up first. Our tactic with Carbide is always hit the disc. As crazy as that sounds if you keep hitting the weapon it will eventually fail.

SEASON 9 CHAMPION

The Grand Final of Season 9 was an electrifying battle between the meanest machine around, Carbide against Eruption. It was a combat between two heavyweights, each determined to smash each other to its death.

CARBIDE

WEIGHT	████████
SPEED	███████
ATTACK	████████
ARMOUR	██████

ERUPTION

WEIGHT	████████
SPEED	████████
ATTACK	███████
ARMOUR	███████

VS

Winner:

CARBIDE

Dream Team:
Dave Moulds (captain, driver, builder and designer),
Sam Smith (weapons operator, builder and designer)

Team Lowdown:
Dave won the UK robot-heavyweight title at the age of 17 and Sam grew up making go-karts in his shed. Deciding to combine their engineering genius, they went on to take three months to build one of the strongest robots in Robot Wars history.

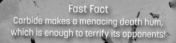
Fast Fact
Carbide makes a menacing death hum, which is enough to terrify its opponents!

HIGHLIGHTS OF CARBIDE'S SEASON 9 JOURNEY

The Qualifiers: Carbide sliced, smashed and slammed Meggamouse, Trolley Range and Crackers 'n' Smash. Carbide was on a mission to kill.

Head-to-Heads: sending sparks flying, Carbide tore off Apollo's side-panel and got its revenge for losing out in series 8. Next up was Crackers 'n' Smash. With a powerful blow, Carbide sent Smash ploughing into the side of the arena with so much force a wall panel came off and play was stopped.

Grand Final: in a frenzied head-to-head, Carbide power-slammed into Aftershock sending part of its armour smashing into the arena wall, piercing right through the polycarbonate glass. Is there no end to Carbide's destruction?

In the final battle, Carbide ripped chunks from Eruption causing extreme mutilation. With one final slam sending Eruption to be wiped out by the arena spikes, Carbide smashed its way to victory. An unstoppable force!

SPEED ROUND WITH DAVE MOULDS

"Carbide's performance throughout the series was better than even we expected and we can't wait to come back in Season 10 to defend our trophy. After the disappointment of getting to the final last year and losing to Apollo, we were very nervous when we found out we would have to fight another flipper in the final.

Eruption is a great machine but we are delighted to have come out on top this time around."

Did you know?
Carbide returned for Season 9 with upgraded internals and enough pushing power to smash an engine block in half with one hit.

WITH THE ROBOTEERS

Behind the scenes, the roboteers are constantly working, fixing, solving problems, testing stuff out. It's all about trial and error in the Pits. Here are some backstage stories from the frontline of roboteering.

WIRE IT UP

Roboteering Trivia #1
Did you know Team Razer has won more battles than any robot in the history of Robot Wars? That is one mean chunk of metal!

Robot: Wyrm

Roboteers:
Nicholas White, Fhiannon McIvor, Jonathan Young

Wyrm's team captain finds himself in a load of bother when a last-minute repair goes horribly wrong. With two minutes to go before a fight, the team realizes the robot has been wired up incorrectly. When the lads press forwards on their transmitter their robot goes backwards. There's no time for a rewiring job so the team comes up with an ingenious solution: flip the transmitter upside down so the bot drives the right way. Problem solved!

Roboteering Trivia #2
Did you know Team Rapid spent £25,000 to build their bot? Let's hope this machine doesn't get bashed to bits!

Robot: **Thor**

Roboteer:
Jason Marston

After giving unreliable performances in Seasons 6 and 7, roboteer Jason Marston knew Thor was capable of more. Ripping up the original designs, Jason went back to work creating a new wrecking machine. Replacing the traditional hammer with a high-speed bladed axe, increasing its speed to 48 kph and using hardened steel for its armour, Thor was ready to go. Reaching fourth place in Season 8 shows how determination and creative thinking gets major results in Robot Wars.

TEST YOUR KNOWLEDGE

Do you have what it takes to be a roboteer?
Complete this quiz to find out, and then total up your scores.

1. Which three robots from the list below made it into the final of Season 9?

Eruption   Terror Turtle   Rusty   Carbide   Apollo   Rapid

2. Name these weapons correctly to pick up maximum points.

_____   _____   _____

3. Aside from the House Robots, name the four hazards in the arena.

_____

_____

_____

_____

4. Name two different ways you could power a robot.

_____

5. What is the maximum weight limit for a robot?

_____ ▢

6. What is a 'kill switch'?

_____ ▢

7. Which three weapons from the list below are forbidden in Robot Wars?

Flail Chain   Fire   Explosives   Multiple Spikes   Strobe Lights   ▢

8. If a robot has a high ground clearance, which weapon should it avoid?

_____ ▢

9. Which robot caused the ultimate upset in series 8
by flipping three of the House Robots?

_____ ▢

10. What is a clusterbot?

_____ ▢

Maximum 3 pts

Total score:

ADD THEM UP!
Quiz Answers on page 171

0-6 points: Re-charge and re-boot
Nice try, but you're still on standby until you can arm yourself with the knowledge
you need to enter the arena. Take five to refresh your mind then try again.
A true roboteer never gives up!

7-12: Caution! New roboteer on the scene
One to watch. You have enough robot knowledge to take the next step, but you still
have a lot to learn. Get yourself prepared for battle!

13-20: 3, 2, 1 ... ACTIVATE!
Wow, with your knowledge you are ready to become a killing machine. Knowledge
is power and your power will send the other bots rolling into the wall. SMASH!

SHARE YOUR KNOWLEDGE

TOP MOST DESTRUCTIVE ROBOTS

There are loads of menacing, metal-crunching robots ready to scare their opponents into submission, but which machines do you think stirred up the ultimate amount of chaos in the battle zone? Write down your top destructive bots in the Robot Wars competition.

Robot name: _____

Weapon: _____

Most destructive moment: _____

_____

_____

WARNING:
DO NOT
RELEASE
OUTSIDE OF
THE ARENA

Robot name: _____

Weapon: _____

Most destructive moment: _____

_____

_____

Robot name: _____

Weapon: _____

Most destructive moment: _____

_____

_____

Robot name: _____

Weapon: _____

Most destructive moment: _____

_____

_____

_____

Robot name: _____

Weapon: _____

Most destructive moment: _____

_____

_____

Robot name: _____

Weapon: _____

Most destructive moment: _____

_____

_____

Robot name: _____

Weapon: _____

Most destructive moment: _____

_____

_____

Robot name: _____

Weapon: _____

Most destructive moment: _____

_____

_____

SHARE YOUR KNOWLEDGE

TOP KNOCKOUTS

As well as causing damage and destruction in the arena, when the robots go for the kill and immobilize their opponents, it's game over for the loser. Write down your top knockout moments of immobilization.

Robot name: _____

Opponent name: _____

Knockout moment: _____

_____

_____

SENDING YOU HOME IN A CARRIER BAG!

Robot name: _____

Opponent name: _____

Knockout moment: _____

_____

_____

Robot name: _____

Opponent name: _____

Knockout moment: _____

_____

_____

Robot name: _____

Opponent name: _____

Knockout moment: _____

_____

_____

Robot name: _____

Opponent name: _____

Knockout moment: _____

_____

_____

Robot name: _____

Opponent name: _____

Knockout moment: _____

_____

_____

Robot name: _____

Opponent name: _____

Knockout moment: _____

_____

_____

RW TIP:
FLIP BACK
THROUGH TO
PAGES 124-129
IF YOU NEED
REMINDING OF
SOME TERRIFYING
KNOCKOUT ACTION!

Robot name: _____

Opponent name: _____

Knockout moment: _____

_____

_____

SHARE YOUR KNOWLEDGE

FAVOURITE ROBOTS

Every fan has their favourite Robot Wars machine. Maybe it's the robot with the craziest design, the sharpest tactics, the most terrifying weapons, or it could be the bot that came back from the brink to send its opponent crashing into the pit of doom. Whatever your criteria, there's a bot for everyone. Write down your favourite robots.

Robot name: _____

What makes it so good? _____

_____

_____

RW TIP:
YOUR FAVOURITES DON'T ALL HAVE TO BE THE STRONGEST OR THE BEST. THE UNDERDOGS OF THE COMPETITION CAN BE JUST AS ENTERTAINING!

Robot name: _____

What makes it so good? _____

_____

_____

Robot name: _____

What makes it so good? _____

_____

_____

Robot name: _____

What makes it so good? _____

_____

_____

Robot name: _____

What makes it so good? _____

_____

_____

Robot name: _____

What makes it so good? _____

_____

_____

Robot name: _____

What makes it so good? _____

_____

_____

Robot name: _____

What makes it so good? _____

_____

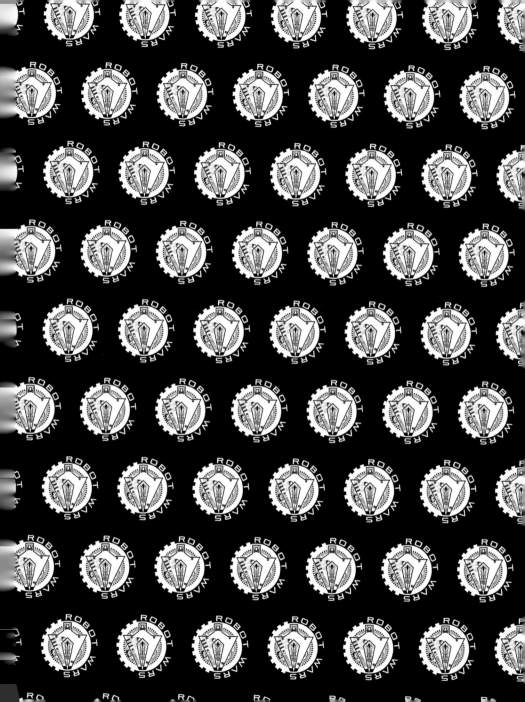

THE BUILD

THE OFFICIAL BUILD RULES

The arena is a dangerous place to be. With so much bashing, slamming, flipping and slicing, some serious build rules need to be in place. Stick to the rules and the robots will have a smashing time. Bend the rules and the bots won't even get to see the arena floor.

Get the lowdown of dos and don'ts below, but for the full list of Robot Wars build rules, visit www.robotwars.tv/media/1243/robot-wars-build-rules.pdf

THE RULES

GENERAL

All competitors build their robots at their own risk. Robot Wars is DANGEROUS.

Robots should only be activated in the arena or testing areas under the guidance of Robot Wars and its safety officials.

When not in the arena or testing areas, all sharp edges and weapons must be covered by safety covers.

WEIGHT IT UP

- Maximum weight: *110 kg*
- Maximum height: *1.2 m*
- Maximum width: *1.5 m*
- Maximum length: *2 m*

Maximum weight also includes all consumables, such as CO_2 gas.

Failure to stick to these sizes means the roboteer will have to strip their robot right back or it will not be allowed to enter the arena.

All robots must include an active weapon, which is designed to damage, immobilize or cause serious destruction to the opponent's robot.

MOVING AROUND

Dos:
- Rolling: on wheels or the entire robot can roll
- Walking: such as using linear-actuator operated legs
- Shuffling: mechanisms such as rotational-cam operated legs
- Ground effect air cushions: such as a hovercraft
- Jumping and hopping

Don'ts:
Robots cannot use exposed rotating-aerofoil, rocket or jet propulsion.
These methods are way too dangerous – even for the
craziness of the Robot Wars arena!

RADIO CONTROLS

Radio systems MUST NOT cause
disturbance to other frequency users.

Only 2.4 ghz DSS (Digital Spread Spectrum) frequencies
are allowed for controlling your robot.

All robots that have dangerous weapons and drive MUST
have a device to instantly switch them to the 'off'
or 'zero' position. This is the 'Kill Switch'.

AUTONOMOUS / SEMI-AUTONOMOUS ROBOTS
(robots that do not need human controls
for one or more of their functions)

Any autonomous robot must be able to be remotely armed and disarmed.

A visible light must be switched on when the robot is in autonomous mode.

When in deactivation mode, autonomous functions should be switched off.

If damage occurs to the disarming component, the robot will
automatically deactivate four minutes after being activated.

THE OFFICIAL BUILD RULES

ELECTRICAL POWER

All robots must include a quick and easy way to turn
off all power to weapons and drive systems without
putting the person switching it off in danger.

If the robot has an internal combustion engine,
the power cut-off link must be labelled 'Kill'.

Robots that can be driven inverted (upside down), must have a power-off
switch on both sides so it can be disarmed when it is either way up.

All robots must have a 'power on' light so it is clear
when the robot has been activated.

Voltages must not exceed 75 V for direct current
or 50 V for alternating current.

BATTERY POWER

Batteries should be protected inside the body shell
to stop them getting punctured or coming loose in combat.

Only use batteries that cannot spill or spray any of their contents when
inverted. Standard car and motorcycle wet-cell batteries are NOT allowed.

Approved battery chemistry: NiCd (Nickel-cadmium), NiMH (Nickel-metal
Hydride), Pb (Sealed Lead Acid), LiFePo4 (Lithium Iron Phosphate),
LiPo (Lithium Polymer).

Leaving LiPo batteries unattended when charging is dangerous
and may result in the robot being removed from the wars.

INTERNAL COMBUSTION ENGINES

The fuel tank must be protected against punctures.

All engines must have a method of remotely shutting off.

Any robot with liquid fuel and oil should be designed not to leak when inverted.

WEAPONS: KEEP THE FIRE OUT

Heat and fire are not allowed to be used as weapons.

This includes:
- No flammable liquids or gases
- No explosives
- No smoke or light weapons that interfere with the viewing of a competitor, a judge, an official or a viewer
- No external laser lights or bright strobe lights

OTHER WEAPONS

Spinning weapons must slow down to a complete stop in under 60 seconds.

Hardened steel blades that could shatter are not allowed.

Maximum length of any rope, chain, wire or similar materials is 1 m.

All high-speed, weapons must have a secure lock to keep them in place.

Sign your name at the bottom of the page if you
agree to stick to these rules ... and remember:

RULE BREAKERS WILL BE ELIMINATED!

I hereby agree to honour the
Robot Wars Build Rules

_____
(sign here)

THE BUILD

STARTING OUT

Check out this advice on how to GET GOING with your build.

Watch the show

Get inspiration and ideas from all the mind-blowing robots that have starred in the Robot Wars competition. Take note of why some robots crash out in the early stages and why others take the arena by storm. Is it down to materials, design, weapon choices, driving skills? You can learn a whole lot about roboteering from observing the bots in action.

Select your team

Although you can brave it alone, building robots is all about teamwork. Choose your crew by finding people with different strengths. Think about the skills you'll need to get your robot battle-ready:

Welding | Electrics | Engineering | Design

Driving | Mechanics | Budgeting | Building | Project managing

Put a team together that can deliver!

Get designing

Put pen to paper. Sketch some designs and plan your weapons to see how your ideas will work. Here are a few handy design hints:

- Is your robot unique? Nobody likes a clone. Give it a personality to make it stand out from the rest.

- Be imaginative and think outside the box.

- Remember to check out the Robot Wars Build Rules for restrictions of weight and size.

- Try out a few different designs before you decide on a final one. It's much easier (and way cheaper!) to rip up a piece of paper and start over than it is to smash up a robot and re-build.

Research

HOW will you build your robot? Investigate what tools you are going to need and work out how you are going to learn any new skills needed for the build: YouTube and online forums are filled with amazing tutorials. Don't be put off if you don't know how to do something, you can easily learn!

WHAT materials will you choose? Think about battery-types, armour, wheels, weapons and power sources.

WHERE will you do your build? Remember, the Robot Wars machines are pretty big so you'll need a safe space to store your tools and create your bot.

Costs

Not the most exciting part, but it's totally necessary to nail your budget. You don't want to get started only to have to abandon your bot due to lack of cash. Robot-building is not cheap, but there are ways to cut costs:

Find yourself a good scrapyard - you'll have to dig through a whole lot of rubbish, but there might just be that perfect piece of grade-5 titanium waiting to be discovered.

Blag, blag, blag! Talk the talk and get sponsorship or convince friends and businesses to give you free or cheap materials. It's amazing what you can get with a bit of blagging.

Most of all - BE CONFIDENT. There has never been a better time to be a roboteer!

THE BUILD

BRAINSCAN WITH
THE ROBOTEERS

It's time to fuel your own creative genius by getting up close
with the experts themselves - the Robot Wars roboteers.

IN THE ZONE WITH TEAM APOLLO

How long did it take you to build Apollo?

Apollo is now in its second generation. Each robot takes about
two months to build, but a lifetime to perfect and maintain.

What was your favourite part of the build?

The design. There is no other challenge that gets you thinking
as creatively as Robot Wars.

Apollo is a force of power in the arena.
What do you think makes your robot so destructive?

The combination of a strong weapon and strong armour. Most robots have one or
the other. We have managed to find the perfect combination to make sure Apollo
can take a beating more than most, but also keep fighting with
its awesome flipper.

IN THE ZONE WITH TEAM ERUPTION

How long did it take you to build Eruption?

Originally it took around nine months to build, but since then we have been continually repairing and upgrading it, to the point where we have lost track of how much time it has taken!

What was the hardest part of the build?

Building the gearboxes was the most difficult and time-consuming part. We built our own custom gearboxes and we spent a lot of time making them really tough and lining everything up correctly.

What was your favourite part of the build?

Assembling Eruption for the final time before its first ever fight was a very satisfying moment. After all the months of work it was finally done and we got to use it in the arena for the very first time!

147

THE BUILD

TOP OF THE BOTS

There is no magic formula for building a winning robot. Roboteering is mostly about using your imagination, making mistakes and then fixing, improving and evolving. But there are some sure-fire ways to get the best out of your bot before you go into battle.

Countdown to Combat

5. Test, test, test! Once your build is ready, test out the weapons, the drive, the strength. You don't want any surprises in the arena.

4. Can your robot self-right if it gets flipped? If not, fix it. Otherwise you could be sent spinning home before you've had a chance to unleash your fury.

3. Are the sensitive electrical components protected? You want to keep them safe from damage during an attack, so bury them deep.

2. Will the armour you have chosen withstand the relentless pounding from opponents? If not, dump and replace.

1. Keep your cool in the arena. Don't be intimated, BE INTIMIDATING!

Analysis: TR2

Time to zoom in for a rapid build-analysis of one of the toughest bots from Season 8 to see what made this machine stand up to the test and reach the semi-final.

Armour

With 3.2 mm HARDOX wear-resistant steel and 20 mm high-density polyethylene panels, it can hold up to some serious thrashing.

Deadly Drive

Awesome driving skills give this bot the edge in the arena. Hard to catch and hard to dodge!

Extra Pain

Red spikes on its sides designed to cause carnage when going for a spin.

Bum Axe!

Spike axe on its rear works in tandem with the flipper meaning it can attack from both sides. DEADLY!

Pneumatic Flipper

Strong and effective, an awe-inspiring weapon that tosses bots around like they are soft toys!

YOUR TEAM, YOUR ROBOT

Okay, so you're ready to become a roboteer? Before you start, you're going to need a plan. Take a look at this questionnaire and fill it out with all your metal-munching ideas. It's the perfect place to bring your initial build ideas to life.

Team name:

_____

Captain:

_____

Who's in your team? (Maximum 4 members)

_____

_____

_____

_____

Robot name:

_____

Type of robot:

Standard ☐　　　Clusterbot ☐　　　Shuffler ☐　　　Walker ☐

Lethal weapon:

Spinner ☐　　　Flipper/Lifter ☐　　　Crusher/Gripper ☐　　　Axe ☐

Other _____

Any other weapons? List them here:

_____

Robot power:

Electric ☐　　Pneumatic ☐　　Hydraulic ☐　　I/C ☐　　Other ☐

Describe your robot in 5 words:

_____

_____

Battery type (including voltage):

_____

Armour:

_____

Flip the page to finish up your plan!

YOUR TEAM, YOUR ROBOT

Speed:

_____

Robot you would most like to battle in the arena:

_____

Robot you would least like to battle in the arena:

_____

Use these bars to show the slam power and
flipper strength of your robot.

Slam Power

|_____|

Pretty weak   Causing chaos   Slamming them
                                                         to pieces

Flipper Strength

|_____|

Firmly on the ground   Flip them up high   Smash them out
                                                         of the arena

Now you've worked out how you want to build your robot, let's see how it's going to look. Use the grid paper to sketch a design for your machine. Add labels to show its weapons, armour and anything else that makes your robot unique.

NOTEBOOK

This section is for you to scribble down ideas, sketch designs, take notes, make lists, calculate costs ... whatever you need to record when planning your build.

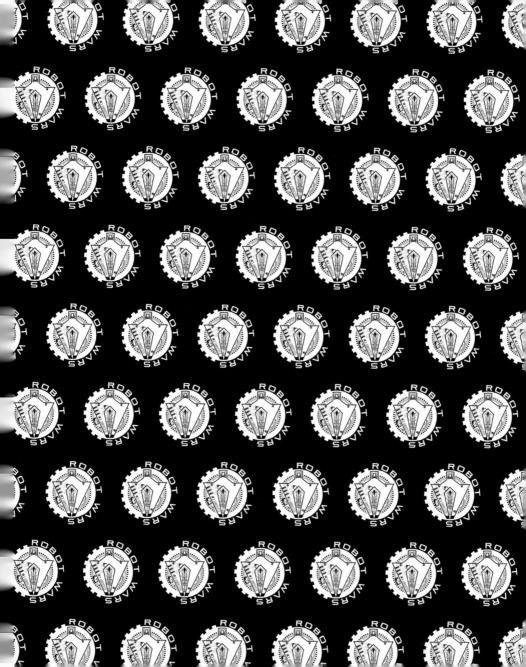

GLOSSARY,
ANSWERS
& INDEX

GLOSSARY

Ah Ampere hour.

Amp Ampere - a unit of electric current.

Aggression Robots that consistently take the battle to their opponents.

Arena Large purpose-built area that is used to host the robot battles.

Arena Spikes Major hazard whereby five spikes rise up from the arena floor.

Autonomous To navigate and manoeuvre without the need for human control.

Control Demonstrating good driving skills and weapon accuracy throughout the battle.

Chassis The frame on which the main parts of the machine are built.

Clusterbot Two or more robots that enter the arena together as one, before splitting and fighting separately.

cm Centimetre.

CO₂ Carbon dioxide.

CPZ Control panel zone.

Damage Causing clear damage to an opponent both visually and internally.

Drive System The part of an engine or mechanical device that makes a machine move.

Flame Pit Major hazard whereby flames shoot out of the arena floor.

Floor Flipper Major hazard whereby a flipper emerges from the arena floor, with the power to chuck robots into the air.

Fog of War A major hazard, which fills the arena with dense fog for 10 seconds.

Group Battle A fight in which four robots battle it out to get through to the next stage of the competition.

Head-to-Head When the top two robots from each group battle fight it out to get to the next round.

Heat Final When the two robots with the most points from the Head-to-Head battles fight against each other to decide who will enter the Grand Final.

House Robots The show's own menacing robots, used to causing chaos and destruction in the arena.

Horsepower A unit of power.

Hydraulic Mechanism activated by liquid pressure.

I/C Intergrated Circuit.

Immobilized When a machine is motionless for more than 10 seconds, it is eliminated.

Internal Combustion Engine An engine which mixes burning fuel and an oxidizer to create high-temperature gases.

kg Kilogram.

Knockout When a robot is out of the game by immobilization, getting flipped over the arena wall or being tipped into the Pit of Oblivion.

kph Kilometres per hour.

LiFePo4 Lithium Iron Phosphate.

LiPo Lithium Polymer.

m Metre.

mm Millimetre.

NiCd Nickel-cadmium.

NiMH Nickel-metal Hydride.

Pb Sealed Lead Acid.

Polycarbonate Strong bulletproof glass used in the arena roof and walls.

Pit of Oblivion Major hazard whereby the arena floor opens up to reveal a deadly hole.

Pits An area where the teams prepare their robots for battle.

Pneumatic A machine operated by air or gas under pressure.

psi Pounds per square inches.

Roboteer A person who designs, creates and drives robots.

rpm Revolutions per minute.

Semi-autonomous A robot that can partially control a weapon or movement without human control.

Torque A force that causes rotation.

tps Times per second.

Trench An area around the arena where robots are tossed into if they are flipped over the wall.

Thwackbot Robots who attack by spinning on the spot.

V Volt.

Viewing Tower A room above the arena protected by bullet-proof glass that teams use to drive their robots.

W Watts

Walker Robots who use legs or feet rather than wheels or tracks.

ANSWERS

1. Eruption, Carbide and Apollo

2. Vertical Spinner, Axe, Crusher

3. Pit of Oblivion, The Flame Pit, Floor Flipper, Arena Spikes

4. Pneumatic, Electric

5. 110 kg

6. A switch labelled 'KILL' that is used to cut a robot's power immediately

7. Fire, Explosives, Strobe Lights

8. A flipper could easily get underneath and send the robot spinning up into the air

9. Apollo

10. A clusterbot consists of two or more robots, rather than one. They enter the arena together as one machine, before splitting and fighting separately

INDEX

Aftershock **16, 43, 124, 127**
Androne 4000 **44**
Apex **45**

Beast **48**
Behemoth **49**
Big Nipper **50**

Carbide 16, 33, 33, 124-7, 130
Cherub 54
Chimera 55
Chimera 2 56
Chompalot 57
Cobra 58
Concussion 59
Coyote 60
Crackers 'n' Smash 61
Crank-E 62
Crazy Coupe 88 39, 63
Crushtacean 64

Dantomkia 65
Dead Metal 38-9
Disconstructor 66
Donald Thump 67
Draven 68

Eruption 35, 69, 123, 126-7, 130, 147
Expulsion 70

Foxic 71
Frostbite 72

Gabriel 73
General, The 74
Glitterbomb 75

Heavy Metal 76
High-5 77
Hobgoblin 78
house robots 24

Infernal Contraption 79
Iron Awe 6 80
Ironside 3 81

Jellyfish 82

Kan-Opener 83
Kegs, The 84
Kill-E-Crank-E 85
King B Remix 37, 86, 123

Magnetar 87
Matilda 26, 36-7
Meggamouse 88
M.R. Speed Squared 89
MS Nightshade 90

Nuts 91
Nuts 2 92

Orte 93
Overdozer 94

Pits, the 122-3
PP3D 95
Pulsar 96
Push to Exit 97

Rapid 98, 129, 130
Razer 99, 128
rules 140-3
Rusty 100, 130

Sabretooth 101
scoring 24-5
Shockwave 16, 102
show format 20-3
Shunt 34-5
Sir Killalot 32-3
Storm 2 103
Supernova 104
Swarm, The 105
Sweeney Todd 106

Tauron 107
Terrorhurtz 108
Terror Turtle 109, 130
Thermidor 2 110
Thor 111, 125, 129
TMHWK 112
Tough as Nails 113
Tracktion 114
TR2 115, 149
Trolley Rage 116

WYRM 117, 128

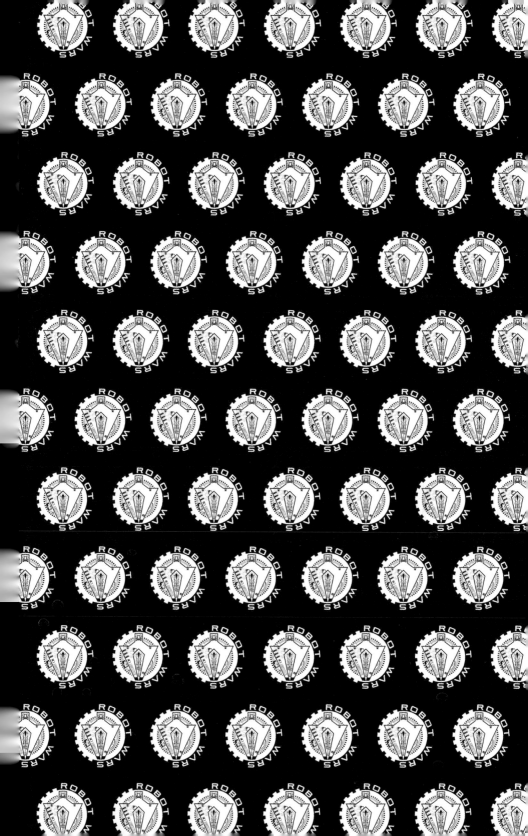